FROM ISAAN TO PATTAYA

ALSO BY PHIL HALL

FROM ISAAN TO PATTAYA

PHIL HALL

TABLE OF CONTENTS

FOR READERS – NOTE ABOUT POINT OF VIEW FORMAT

As this book contains so many characters and many of them being pivotal to the story, I decided to ditch the traditional first or third person format.

Instead I have given the point of view from each character where I feel it is relevant.

Of course, Ice is the main protagonist and she gets the majority of the narrative here but there are insights from other characters that, I feel, would not be possible to get across without using this unorthodox format.

I hope you agree 😊

PROLOGUE

Ban Mee, Buriram Province

The Isaan sun shone so brightly onto the classroom whiteboard that it was impossible to follow the characters that the teacher had scrawled out earlier. With over 50 children in the cramped room, the temperature was hot enough to cook an egg in minutes.

At the back of the class sat a pretty female student who was day dreaming her way through the one hour lesson.

She would have preferred to be almost anywhere than in this classroom right now.

Her imagination was bright and vivid as she pictured herself being swept off her feet by a very handsome foreign man. He resembled one of the more famous movie stars, was it Johnny Depp, or perhaps Brad Pitt?

He took her to a world where the doldrums of school and rules to be followed didn't exist.

She sighed out loud and even the teacher heard her over the creaky noise of the ceiling fan:

'If only I could live that life…'

As the teacher removed her from the classroom and ordered her to report to the detention room for the third time that week, he gave her some sage advice that she would only understand many years later:

'Be careful what you wish for, Ice…'

PART I – HUMBLE BEGINNINGS

CHAPTER ONE — HOMETOWN GIRL

Nong Khai, North Eastern Thailand, 2018

'Please, please let us go!'

The two young Thai girls were begging for their lives, but they weren't having any luck.

Chained up in the back of the large van, they were being thrown around like rag dolls, their slender frames hurled from pillar to post every time the vehicle hit a pothole.

The man tasked with driving was anxiously peering into the rear-view mirror, and although his accelerator foot was flat to the floor, the police car was almost level. When the first gunshots were heard, he yelled out a command to his colleague, who was struggling to hang on for dear life. This wasn't the first time the pair had been pursued by the Boys in Brown, and it probably wouldn't be the last, but this time they had precious cargo.

The standard escape plan would be to open the rear doors of the van and kick out whoever they had caught, usually resulting in at least one death, but at least their pursuers would stop long enough for them to get away.

Except these two girls had attributes that made them worth the risk.

They were not only virgins, but also identical twins. This was most men's fantasy and neither Kwan nor Somluk were ready to let go of that prize just yet.

Kwan did his best to take a last-minute right-hand turn and almost lost control of the Toyota.

The sisters were again hurled across the length of the rear compartment, only this time Kwan heard the rear doors open and the unmistakable sound of bodies hitting the road. He almost slammed on the brakes.

'Somluk, what the hell have you just done, you idiot?!'

Slamming the doors shut, Kwan's literal partner in crime sighed as their pursuer gave up the chase.

He replied breathlessly:

'Thanks to your shitty driving, both bitches are dead. Their necks snapped like twigs, so fuck you too!'

He scrambled over the seat to ride shotgun, offered Somluk a cigarette as they chatted mournfully about that big pay packet that had just blown them both off.

With no thought to the double homicide that they had caused, it was time for the Chicken Farm Crew to hit the next village for whatever poor soul was in their cross-hairs next.

⁕⁕⁕

Ban Mee, Buriram Province

Ice

It was around my seventeenth birthday when I realised that I was being treated differently compared to my sisters. The school term was just around the corner and although I disliked education, I was excited to start *Mathayom Five[1]* at our village school. According to my elders, Mathayom Five was when students were finally allowed to have a voice. Puberty-fuelled antics were on every student's mind and physical interaction with the opposite, or, in some cases, the same, sex was on the menu. But when Mum and Dad drove off to the city with my sisters in order to buy school uniform, I was left behind.

It was the way in Isaan that conversations about big issues were usually swept under the table. I knew better than to argue, and

---

1   *Mathayom Five - School year for 16/17 year olds in Thailand.*

instead of making this annual trip, I was given a list of domestic duties to carry out.

My education had ended abruptly.

I was trying to deal with this when my thoughts were interrupted by a loud voice:

'Ice! What are you doing today?'

I looked up to see the slightly handsome face of Bank, my 27-year-old neighbour. He was puffing on a fake Marlboro cigarette, the aroma made me feel dizzy even though he was ten metres away.

I explained that I was coming to terms with the fact that my youth was over, and instead of ignoring me as Thai men normally did, he handed me a cigarette and offered me a light.

I drew on the Marlboro and before I could exhale, I started coughing my guts up. Bank put his hand on my back and gently slapped as I was struggling for air.

'First time, hey?'

I decided on a second attempt. This time my lungs were semi-braced for the smoke and it felt better.

I noticed that Bank's hand was still on my back, so decided to take a step away.

'Do you want to earn some money, *Nong Sao*?'[2]

I shook my head, intent on finishing the cigarette without any more loss of face.

Bank beckoned for me to follow him and led me to his pickup just outside his house. We were far too poor to own such a vehicle. Mum, Dad and my two sisters had taken our ramshackle motorbikes, our only means of transportation, into Buriram.

The heat was already well into the +30°C territory, par for the course during April in Isaan, and I was sweating as if I'd been doing some strenuous activity, not just taken a shot of nicotine.

'I need an assistant to sell these watermelons, interested?'

---

2 *Nong Sao* - Literal translation is 'Younger Sister'.

There wasn't much else on offer and money was always tight for me. I forgot about the mundane list of chores, so I agreed. We struck a deal that would see me receive 100 baht for a day's work and off we went.

Although still a young girl, my breasts had doubled in size over the last six months and this transformation had not gone unnoticed by Bank. In fact, it hardly went unnoticed by any man who had a conversation with me. I caught him having a sly peek more than once during the ten-minute journey to his roadside stall.[3]

***

Nong Kai Province

Somluk

I've been working for the CFC, Chicken Farm Crew, for the last twenty years, and it never fails to surprise me. Okay, technically we are no more than sex traffickers, but a job is a job, right? Apart from a few things, the remit hasn't changed during these two decades. For each girl we bring into *The Industry*,[4] we get paid ten thousand baht, that amount has remained the same. The method that we use to snare these girls is totally on us. No questions are asked and so long as the buyer gets no heat from the police, they couldn't care

---

3   *For those who have travelled around Thailand, these roadside stalls are a common site between cities and towns. Typically, they will sell almost identical goods that are from that area of Thailand. Fruit, hot and cold food and even silk cushions are amongst the usual goods. It may seem odd to have exactly the same items for sale from neighbouring stalls, but this is Thailand and every stall holder seems to make a living. Almost always on major roads, these are usually free of rent and offer a welcome detour for motorists travelling through a mostly uninteresting countryside.*

4   *Known simply as 'The Industry', prostitution in Thailand employs an estimated one million people, and these include many professions. Pattaya is the centre of the red-light scene in Thailand but there are many other cities and towns that have brothels and bars that cater for every mal, and female need. It's a sad fact that human sex trafficking is still a major concern and the likes of the Chicken Farm Crew are supplying this demand in the cruellest way possible. Some say that the girls are far from forced into this role, it's a choice that they make. But that doesn't include those that are kidnapped at force and sometimes sold into brothels as sex slaves.*

less.

If the girl is a virgin, we get another ten thousand and if she isn't beautiful, we may have to barter to a lower price. We try our best not to bruise the girls when we beat them, but that isn't always possible. In some parts of the country, we offer the family a nominal sum, usually one thousand baht or less. Or if we happen upon an attractive girl in the border towns, where law is a stranger, we'll use a little force and some drugs to get them into our van.

Recent times have seen a few changes, especially with regards to social media, mobile phones and other technological advances. This is why we try and avoid high profile snatches and steer clear of the bigger cities.

It's just me and Kwan who do the legwork - our boss, a formidable lady called Wannee, makes much more than the pair of us together, but that will change soon. We are saving up to start our own business. The only problem with this plan is that Kwan seems incapable of maintaining any savings. The fact that he's an alcoholic, and a drug addict, probably doesn't help.

Kwan

I was still really pissed off that we had lost out on those twins yesterday. They were around fifteen, perhaps a little old for some of our clients, but both beauties and identical twins. What was not to like?

That old Chinese man in Bangkok was interested and he would have paid many thousands of baht for their pretty arses. This time around I would have saved at least half of my bounty and then would have partied for the next week. More than likely I would have ended up somewhere in Cambodia, where sex and drugs are cheap and practically legal. Then the next mission would start, and I'd meet back up with Somluk to work on the list that the old whore down in Pattaya would email to us.

I'm not scared of anyone but Wannee. Let's just say that her bark is definitely not as dangerous as her venomous bite.

They say that she poisoned her first four husbands, and that she also cut off each poor bastard's dick and fed it to her pet crocodile for them to watch as they exhaled their last few breaths. I'm surprised that evil beast hasn't met a similar fate, but the rumours are that Wannee and the hideous reptile are actually lovers.

Makes my skin crawl, I can tell you.

Thankfully, Kwan and I are still in her good books – well, at least that was the case until the twin incident.

She wants to see us both tomorrow.

I will not sleep well tonight, but at least I have a few pills to help me.

***

Thepprasit Road, Jomtien, near Pattaya

Wannee

Those stupid idiots are going to pay for their mistake. I already took a deposit for the twins from Nong Kai and now it's all going back to that fat Chinese pervert in the capital. My spies on the Lao border had been watching them for months, and now that's all gone down the toilet.

Kwan and Somluk are starting to get sloppy, one more mistake and that's their lot. My sweet reptilian soulmate has been yearning for more human flesh, so at least he's going to be happy.

I've owned Samart for 20 years and, unlike other males, he always does what he's told. I keep him fed on stray dogs and cats, but it's human flesh that he yearns for.

Maybe he'll be able to scratch that itch again sooner rather than later.

Ban Mee, Buriram Province

Ice

Selling watermelons was definitely not my dream career, but I wanted to show my family that at least I had some value and could help us earn a living, especially after the abrupt end of my education path.

The day had dragged on, especially as Bank rather quickly ran out of conversation and seemed to be more interested in playing on his iPhone. I was surprised when we sold all of the fruit, and even more so when he handed me an extra 100 baht note as we packed the stall away. Bank had been drinking beer for most of the day, but no matter how concerned I was at his fitness to drive, I couldn't be bothered to point this out as he took us home. I had already learnt that Thai men do not listen to their female counterparts and always seemed to do exactly what they wanted; besides, I desperately needed some rest.

I often overheard Dad lamenting the fact that Mum had sired three girls and would have swapped one of us, probably me, for a boy any day of the week. This hurt me to the core, and for the life of me, I couldn't see why he would do that. Boys were treated like kings, even in poor villages like mine, and girls, well, we were far lower down the rungs of the family ladder.

After Bank parked the car, I walked over to my family home and forced a smile as my sisters were putting on some kind of a fashion show for our parents.

I gave them a swerve and handed my day's wages over to Dad, who continued to look straight on at Bank's truck.

'You little bitch! We gave you a list of jobs to do and you have been out with that bastard next door!'

Before I could answer, the back of his hand hit me full in the face and I sunk to the ground in a heap.

It had always been like this with Dad, he never laid a finger on Nam or Oot yet seemed ready to hit or kick me at the slightest opportunity. I often wondered if I had been blamed for the family's misfortune, yet I did my best to earn a little money whenever I could.

Dad was an engineer up until a few years ago, but when he had that bad accident at work, he was laid off and the insurance payment soon dried up. This was mainly due to his love of gambling on his fighting cocks and his drinking.

It was not an easy realisation and it kept me up at night more than once, but I started to come to terms with the fact that he didn't love me as much as my sisters. When I was finally hauled out of school and I was shown how little my education mattered, that was the moment it finally sank in.

I wasn't loved by him, nor Mum.

I adored my sisters, but even they found it hard to meet my stare after this last humiliation.

I went inside, threw myself on the thin mattress and, not for the first time, cried myself to sleep.

Somchai

Don't get me wrong, I love all three of my girls but sometimes, like right now, I still wish we were blessed with a son, or even two.

Nam, Oot and Ice are great daughters, and each one of them would do anything for me and my wife. But since my accident, I haven't been able to bring in enough money for this family of five. Education is costing so much these days and the decision to take Ice out of school broke my heart. If anything, she is the cleverest of my three daughters and she is also the bravest.

That is the reason why I chose Ice to leave school.

Oot and Nam just aren't strong enough to face the world right now and they need all the help they can get.

Back in my day, further education simply wasn't an option for poor families, and I did just fine when I left at fifteen. I worked my way up the ranks in the local engineering firm and was doing well right up to the accident.

Seeing Ice had spent all day with Bank made my blood boil through my veins, and I slapped her before I realised the intensity of the anger that had washed over me. I couldn't help it – it had nothing to do with any chores, those are there just to keep her on the straight path but knowing Bank and seeing his lustful gaze aimed at Ice, it was too much for me to bear.

That pervert has his eyes on all three of my girls, and I promise, if he touches one of them, I will blow his head off his shoulders… if only I could afford a gun.

I guess my biggest fear is that Ice will end up selling her body to the highest bidder. The shame that would bring to his family would be the last straw. That's exactly what happened to Bot who lives across the village. It was about a year ago when his daughter, Ying, came back from Pattaya and told the whole village that she earnt a living on her back down there.

Okay, she may have bought her parents a shiny new Toyota Hero pickup truck, but what good did that do? The shame nearly finished Bot and his wife. If that wasn't bad enough, she returned six months later with her *farang*⁵ boyfriend. I think he was from England, but he was even older than Bot. Big, fat, bald, sweaty thing he was, and didn't even show the respect to wear smart clothes. No, he was always in a vest with tight shorts, socks and those bloody flip flops. Again, she brough gifts for her parents and sibling, two nice motorbikes and even paid for a new house, twice the size of ours.

This time Bot was a little more accepting and when they announced Ying and Mr Piggy were getting married, I could literally see the baht signs appear in his eyes.

The shame was replaced with wealth, but I wasn't jealous, well not much anyway. No, I would rather kill myself than see Ice work as a prostitute, I would do whatever I could to stop that, so long as it didn't put my other two daughters at risk.

---

5   **Farang** - *Westerner.*

Nong Kai Province

Kwan

I was in an argument with Somluk when I saw her. She had walked in front of our van and, thanks to my amazing driving, I managed to stop in time.

I had never seen such a beautiful thing: long, black hair, pale skin and legs that never ended. She had a smile that suggested a hint of naughtiness, yet when she spoke, it was pure class. This girl was from a wealthy family, which made me want her even more, but the thing that made her so very irresistible was the colour of her eyes.

Instead of the dark brown almond orbs that I was expected, I saw my reflection in a pair of pale sapphire-blue beauties.

She had stumbled onto the tarmac, so I killed the engine and raced out of my seat to offer her a helping hand.

Somluk must have seen the same fascinating features because that bastard was already there doing his impression of a knight in not so shining armour.

The stuck up girl didn't even thank us, and when I took a sneaky photo, she stormed off leaving us with a few choice Isaan swear words ringing in our collective ears.

Somluk

After the beauty had walked away, I looked into my colleague's far less attractive eyes and we both high fived each other before climbing back into the van. There was a spring in my step because instead of heading back to a certain showdown with Wannee and her hideous Crocodile, we may have just found something to save us.

The trip had been a failure - after the death of our precious cargo up in Nong Kai, we'd been chased by the Police, crashed twice and came up empty-handed, apart from that thirteen-year-old tied up in the back of the van. She was decent enough, but still had bad skin and was flatter than the Isaan plains we were currently driving through.

Wannee would not be pleased but now maybe, just maybe, we had something up our sleeves.

***

Ban Mee, Buriram Province

Ying

I made sure that John was asleep before sneaking out of bed to get dressed. I heard the motorbike outside our house and my heart started racing when I recognised the handsome Thai man who was waiting for me.

Boi was everything that John was not.

He had lovely skin, white teeth and incredible abs that made me wet just thinking about them. Sex was just as incredible as his looks, and he could last for hours.

Sleeping with John turned my stomach and for me to bear it, I literally had to lie back and think of everything this kind man had given to me. He may be pig-ugly, but no one can deny his huge heart. I had to keep this pretence up at least until I could figure a way out of this sham of a marriage. I had learnt that once we returned to England, I could divorce him after two years. Boi was happy enough to wait for me but I had a feeling he wouldn't be so patient once I'd flown overseas. He was always hanging around that bitch Yam back in Pattaya and even now, I could smell her cheap perfume on his skin as we sped away from the house.

Forty minutes later, as we lay naked together in his cheap hotel room, none of that mattered because we were alone at last. As usual, the sex was breath-taking and, both of us, drenched in our sweet sweat, promised to see this through because we were going to spend the rest of our lives together. We'd be rich with John's money, and as for that little whore Yam; well, she could go and find a fat old white *buffalo*[6] of her own.

***

Thepprasit Road, Jomtien, near Pattaya

Kwan

When we pulled up outside the boss's plush residence, Kwan and I had a little huddle, just to come up with a plan that could cover our backs when the inevitable took place. Wannee would be ready for us, and I suspect one large crocodile would be licking its lips at the prospect of a human main course. Hustling the girl from the van, we gingerly approached the front door and gave it a loud knock.

We both jumped when it opened almost immediately and were faced with her number one bodyguard. This immediately put us on the back foot as his grim features beamed back at us.

Rambo, as he was known, would only visit the boss when serious shit was going down. He scoffed at our reaction and blocked our paths, simply pointing to the gate at the side of the huge house. We both knew that this path led to her swimming pool and that could only mean one thing: one, or both of us, were going to go for a deadly swim.

Somluk

Well, this plan of Kwan's was already ripped to pieces and flushed down the bloody toilet, as it appeared we were already being led to the Kangaroo, or Crocodile Court, by Rambo. Rumour has it that he actually swims with the crocodile in order to toughen himself up. In fact, it is said that he rescued the creature from a handbag factory somewhere in Laos and the pair of them are actually related.

---

6   **Buffalo/Kwai** – *An insulting term often used for foreign males who pay for sex with Thai prostitutes. It is fairly common for the girl to continue seeing her Thai boyfriend or husband, once the unlikely wedding has taken place. It's even more commonplace for the Thai male to have a string of girlfriends of his own. Fights can and do break out when the Buffalo's money is being requested by the Thai male and the ex-prostitute isn't able to meet these demands. In fact, his money has to go rather a long way if every person in this menage-a-trois/insert figure here, is to be paid for their share in this multi-faceted deceit.*

Anyway, we'd soon find out. We approached the boss, who was knocking back a black soda with some speed.

Wannee

These boys were in for a treat, as today had pissed me off enough already.

The police had raided two of my brothels near the Cambodian border and all 23 girls were currently being held by them. Thankfully, they were second string whores who were already of a legal age. The police were probably only interested in winding me up, and they had already offered to let them back to work, so long as I paid the release fee.

The greedy bastards wanted half a million baht, and as soon as I saw that figure in the text message, I just laughed and went back to my drink. I had already paid their parents, boyfriends or whoever, that amount a few years back when the girls were prettier and actually worth something. The money they earned since had tripled that investment, and as far as I was concerned, they were past their sell-by date and could rot in prison.

Now I'm faced with Kwan, Somluk, and some non-descript girl who looks like she needs a skin graft before any man would spit on her, let alone take her to bed.

'What the fuck do you think this is? Some kind of joke?'

They both responded by looking at the ground until Somluk, the brighter of the two, pushed the girl in my direction.

I shouted at her to sit on the grass by the pool whilst I continued my tirade.

'I gave you one fucking job to do and you can't even get that right! Those twins were worth a lot of money and now you insult me with this underfed wretch!'

I was enjoying this power play and indicated to Rambo to bring the stupid one, Kwan, to the poolside.

Without being told, Rambo then brought the large feeding contraption alongside the hapless employee and used cable ties to secure the poor bastard's arms behind his back. Less than a minute later, Kwan was hoisted over the pool and screaming like a Burmese virgin on her wedding night.

This hadn't gone unnoticed by Samart, who started showing off with his new trick. It had taken a few months to get it right, but the huge beast was able to jump up out of the pool as if he was a rather ugly looking dolphin. His muscular tail propelled the enormous body at least a metre out of the water before belly flopping back in and emptying hundreds of litres of the green liquid into the surrounding grass. I had encouraged this trick by hanging stray dogs, cats or whatever worthless creature over the pool. In this case it was Kwan, and by the look on his face, this was time well spent.

I grew bored of the usual punishment and so far, this was working out nicely. After his second leap, I told Rambo to lower the doomed Kwan within reach as I knew that Samart could only do this two more times before sinking to the floor of the pool.

'Wait, please!'

I looked across to Somluk who dared to move from his place towards me. Rambo let go of the device and instinctively trained his Desert Eagle on Somluk, just waiting for the chance to empty some lead into the fool's chest.

Before allowing him to end Somluk, I noticed that a mobile phone had been thrown towards me. I held up the device to look at the screen with feigned disinterest. Even though the device's screen was now cracked, what I saw was enough for me to have a better look.

There was a beautiful girl, probably about seventeen at most, with incredible hair and skin. I was already dumbfounded, but then I saw a pair of piercing sapphire-blue eyes looking fiercely directly back at me.

It was a five-million-baht vision and, as I placed the phone on the poolside table, I started to feel a warmth inside that could only be fed by potential evil deeds and immeasurable wealth.

Kwan

I had already said my prayers and was ready to meet my maker when a reluctant Rambo wheeled the macabre device away from the pool and released me after Wannee's instructions. That last leap from Samart was too close for comfort, the stench of the rotting flesh from his disgusting mouth hitting me at full pelt as I expected to be snatched into the pool, like a wriggling worm on a baited hook.

But that moment was at least suspended for now and I shuffled back to Somluk with the sound of my heartbeat reverberating through my ears.

We both listened as we were tasked with bringing the blue-eyed beauty back to this evil harridan and sighed with relief as it seemed we were presented with one last chance at redemption.

We'd almost forgotten the kidnapped girl who had decided to stand up and seemed to be trying pathetically to make one last run for her life.

Sadly, it was all in vain, as she was way too close to the pool and slipped over just in time for the dejected Samart to snag her ankles and drag the poor child into his lair for a meal. It was probably just a starter for that fat monster, but food was food.

Wannee seemed almost upset at this vision of horror and shouted out in anger:

'Oh my God, that would have been a brilliant video to send to my friends, but now it's too late!'

This was more like the evil bitch who had paid our salary for the last two decades.

Thanking our lucky stars, Somluk and I stumbled back to the van, muttering empty threats as we weighed up our slim options.

✳✳✳

Ban Mee, Buriram Province

Ying

As usual, my time with Boi came to an end too swiftly and, as I snuck back into my air-conditioned home, I dreamily smelt my palms and the back of my hands to remember his sweet scent

21

before washing it away in the shower.

The next day, after a drawn-out breakfast in bed with too many questions about last night, I started to devise a plan that could bring my precious Boi into my life a little more often.

'Honey, I have a cousin who needs work, he can do anything you want.'

John seemed distracted as he was playing on his phone, but at least he was smiling, or seemed somewhat receptive. After three or four more hints, he agreed that Boi could stay at the house and would be paid 30,000 baht per month for odd jobs and gardening.

How rich and stupid could this man be? If only he realised that the main job Boi would be doing was making sweet love to me… I had to keep a straight face as John went back to his phone.

I was buzzing to let Boi know about my cunning plan but for now, I needed some real Isaan food, and before visiting my parents I stopped off at a noodle shop on the edge of the village.

This family were friends with Mum and Dad, and I had often heard about the delicious noodles that Somchai's wife, Patty, used to make. Apparently, they had decided to relaunch this business, and it was exactly what I needed right now.

It had been months since I spent time with my own family and decided a trip down culinary memory lane was just what we needed. Like most of the family run businesses in the village, they had failed ever since the 7-11[7] had opened on the main road. They just couldn't compete with the opening hours and low prices, especially for small meals and snacks. Some of the poorer kids would just hang around the entrance to the store just to feel the ice-cold air-conditioning wash over them every time the automatic double doors opened.

I eagerly made my way to where the stall was, so I was pretty pissed off to see that it wasn't open, despite the fact it was almost midday. These bumpkins didn't seem to get the fact that they needed to adapt to the current climate if they even had a chance of keeping

---

7   *7-11 – Worldwide chain of convenience stores that appear in almost every road in towns and villages and cities across Thailand.*

afloat.

I had texted my parents to see if they wanted me to wait for these idiots, when I noticed a young girl of about seventeen standing in front of me. She was beautiful and despite wearing no make-up, so gorgeous that it was like looking in a mirror about five years ago.

Her name was Ice. I then remembered babysitting for her and two little brats before I started working the bar in Pattaya.

We made small talk as she cooked the noodles, and I could sense a little interest in my own state of affairs. I was more than happy to share my account of how I have become the richest person the village and offered her a cigarette whilst waiting for my change.

Ten minutes later I was sat cross legged with my family munching on the delicious bowls of noodles and, if only for a few minutes, it was like the good old days, before we were rich. Life was much simpler then, despite the financial hardships, and as we reminisced, I felt a brief fleeting sadness pass over me.

The mood was then cruelly snatched away from us when I received a photo text of Boi's erect manhood held over a backdrop of John and mine's wedding photograph. Making my excuses, I said goodbye to my family and raced back for some passionate sex on the marital bed.

Somchai

I was pleasantly surprised to see Ice opening the noodle stall today, if a little late, and she seemed to be doing a decent job as she served Bot's slut daughter. She seemed at ease in her new role, but I was a little concerned when Ying gave her a cigarette and Ice readily accepted before placing it behind the counter.

Bot had not worked again ever since his daughter had announced that she was now the main breadwinner of the family, and I used to ask Buddha why it was him and not me who had received such good fortune. Of course, he had to pay the price of dealing with jealous neighbours and those looks behind his back, not to mention the shame of losing such massive face when she brought that pink pig into the village.

I guess the new house and motorbikes lessened the blow, but I was sure that given this option, I would never weaken like he did. Although I must say, when he showed me that Apple watch and matching iPad, I was a little shaken, in fact I even looked up the price during my usual session in the internet coffee shop and nearly spilt my cup of chai when I realised the pair were worth more than I could earn in a year.

Had the man no shame?

Ice

Waking up, I realised that today was the beginning of my new career as a noodle chef, a prospect of little excitement to me. As I lazily prepared the ingredients in the kitchen, I heard a motorbike pull up outside the house. I was late and hurried out with the freshly cut herbs and soaked noodles to see Ying, the daughter of Bot, looking angrily and tapping her watch.

Cheeky bitch - this was the girl who had won the Buffalo lottery and she seemed to have forgotten how she had got this prize. I shuddered as I thought of the idea of lying underneath, or more likely, on top of that foul-smelling bald creature every day and night for the rest of her life. To be fair, it was more likely that he would expire first, but this was still a despicable future to have to deal with.

Her facial features softened as she recognised me as the shy girl for whom she baby sat for all those years ago. In fact, Ying was very nice to me, and after we shared small talk, I started to see that she hadn't changed at all. I really wanted to learn more about her but was too polite to ask any prying questions. She asked me if I really planned to waste my life slaving over the noodle store, but I just giggled and changed the subject as she offered me a cigarette. I had no intention of ever smoking it, but decided to accept, as I didn't wish to offend her.

A little later, my family went out for the afternoon, leaving me in charge of the house and the business. I suppose I should have felt a little pride, but my mind kept wandering back to that vision of Ying riding that foreign man mountain in the largest house in my village.

To be honest, sex had never really interested me, although I was starting to have a few wet dreams about my favourite singer, Sek Loso.

When the sun was low in the sky and before my family returned, I closed the stall for the day and counted the takings.

I had slaved away for less than 500 baht, and this was supposed to be the big launch day. I had a few ideas about using social media for promoting the business, but Mum and Dad's eyes just glazed over as I explained how it was vital for us to start a targeted audience campaign on Facebook and Twitter.

During my shower I was sure I heard them return, but as I dried off in front of my fan in my bedroom, I realised that I was still alone.

Still, there was a weird smell hanging in the air, a bit like stale cigarette smoke that lingered just long enough for me to recognise the stench.

'Ice, we are home, how much money did you make today?'

Dad's voice released me from my vivid daydreaming, and I skipped out to meet them, clutching the purple 500 baht note that I had toiled all afternoon for.

End of Chapter One

CHAPTER TWO – CHICKEN FARM CREW HIJINKS

On the road, somewhere in Chonburi Province

Kwan

I was still shell-shocked by how close to death I had been yesterday and was taken by surprise when Somluk stood up for me. He could have easily been killed by Rambo, and yet he stood his ground. Me? I would have buckled and just stayed quiet, as I am the definition of a true coward.

Wannee showed what a bitch she is when she made that joke about the poor kid being eaten by Samart. I never want to get that close to him ever again.

In fact, if this little mission fails, there is no way that I will ever go to Pattaya again because we will be decimated by that foul beast - and I'm talking about the cursed Wannee, not Samart.

Somluk

Kwan seems a little quiet today, I think his near-death experience making its way to him from the jaws of a crocodile shook him up. Hell, he even made a donation to the monks this morning, that is a first for him.

Still, we have one more shot at this, and I'm going to make sure we get that blue-eyed bitch, whatever it takes. We have a six-hour drive before nightfall, which should get us to spitting distance of where Kwan nearly flattened her into the road.

I made a donation as well this morning; we need all the help that we can get for this mission.

Thepprasit Road, Jomtien, near Pattaya

Wannee

With those two idiots off on their trip, I can finally get time for some real work.

The bus from Korat is due in shortly and this is my bread and butter business. In The Industry, this particular bus is known as the 'Farm Fresh Express'. It takes around seven hours from start to finish, and I try to make the daily trip to get the second bus that arrives around midnight. This is always the better option because the girls are usually sleepy and looking for a place to stay.

I bring Rambo and whoever else is available and we do a quick check as they disembark with their bags, and then round up the ones we like the best. Of course, there are other pimps doing the same thing, so we have to be quick. More than once, Rambo has used his gun to dissuade the other bars from grabbing the prime stock. After that, we toss them in the van, starve them for a few days to weaken them enough so they pose less resistance, and sell them off as we see fit.

The scraps are either let loose or, depending on my mood, fed to Samart. He can eat about five in one sitting as they usually weigh no more than 40 kilograms. I don't feel bad, because at least their shitty lives have been of some use, and I'm sure they'll come back in the next one as a more worthy being.

I had some interest just now in the blue-eyed girl from the North. The same old Chinese pervert in Bangkok put in an opening bid of two million baht, so this could be a good project.

Hope those twits manage it this time, how hard can it be?

***

Ban Mee, Buriram Province

Ice

Well, my new job didn't last long. Less than a few days into selling

noodles and we realised that we simply did not have enough customers to make it worthwhile. The 7-11, less than a kilometre away, was selling tasty cheap food at a price that we cannot compete with.

I begged Mum and Dad to let me do some online advertising, but they just don't understand. It would have been easier if we actually had a computer to work on, but I was happy to spend a few hours a day in the internet café doing this for them. Dad thought this was just an excuse for me to play games or chat with friends, he really doesn't have a clue.

I decided to go directly to my competitor and see if 7-11 had a job for me. They did! After a quick interview with the manager, who seemed to be obsessed with my boobs, I was given a trial run and after 30 minutes, the job was mine.

The hours seemed long, but I was guaranteed 300 baht a day and was even allowed one day off every two weeks.

What really pissed me off was Dad's reaction when I came home in the cute uniform. He took one look and just stormed off.

Sometimes I hate him, what the hell can I do to make that damn old man smile?

Bank

I ran into Ying last night at the village bar, and she looked so bloody good!

The bitch all but ignored me, but without my help, well, she would probably be in a low rent brothel or working at the *Tawen Daeng*[1] like all the other failed wannabes. Eventually she came over and did a little *wai*[2] just for me. Her tits looked great but it turns out they are fake, just like her nose and teeth.

Oh well, we had a little chat and I was surprised when she showed a real interest in that little slut next door. Ying was always a smart

---

1   ***Tawen Daeng*** – *Nationwide chain of Thai nightclubs offering food, drink and live music and hostesses for dancing, similar to a western 'Honky Tonk'.*
2   ***Wai*** – *Thai word for bow, to show respect to those in higher positions. Displayed by holding both hands, palms together, by your face. The higher the position of the person who is being waiied, the higher up the hands are held.*

one and it turns out that she has designs of her own on young Ice. Mine were a little more basic, but I did wonder if I could do a deal just like the one that propelled Ying to stardom back in the day? I had connections, and I suspected she had some of her own in Pattaya.

We had a conversation that, although left unfinished, would have made Ice's pretty little ears burn. I decided that I would do my best to get her alone tomorrow and started to hatch a plan, before Ying got there first.

***

Somchai

As if the day couldn't get any worse, first Ice quits the noodle stall business after just half a week and then she goes and gets a job at 7-11.

Doesn't she have any family loyalty? Okay, she will earn nearly 10,000 baht a month, but that just is not the point. The loss of face when my friends and neighbours see her coming home in that blasted uniform, and not to speak of the things they will say behind my back. It is all plenty enough to drive me to drink.

The sight of Bot making his way into the village pub was just the tragically perfect end to an awful day. The little bastard was blinged up as per usual and was even drinking a 7-11 slurpy that was probably served by Ice a few minutes earlier.

Bot

Sure, I was surprised to see that poor cripple Somchai having a beer. How could he afford it these days? Bastard even tried to blank me as I walked up to him and it took a few minutes for him to look up, despite the fact I was wearing my favourite white suit with matching trainers.

'Hey old friend, please allow me to buy you a few beers!'

He couldn't refuse, as I had him in the corner. Still looked a smug bastard, and I knew he was one of the worst gossips when it came

to the source of my wealth.

I was upset when Ying announced she was leaving her job in the Tawen Daeng to move down to Pattaya, but that was soon replaced with pride when the payments started to roll in. Even when Mr Piggy rocked up in his brand-new pick-up truck and handed it over to yours truly, I took a few moments to appreciate the gravity of the situation. We were rich, and all because my daughter was a whore. There was no denying it. I had always considered the people in The Industry to be no more than low-hanging fruit, but there was more to it than originally meets the eye.

This moment was as sweet as any, and as I ordered two more shots of high-end whisky, it sure felt as if I was the King of the World, with Somchai nothing but a puny ant under my 5,000-baht Nike trainers. It was time for much needed payback, and the night was still young.

***

Ying

As Boi walked away, leaving me in a heap on the floor, I had to suddenly re-evaluate what the hell I was doing in this relationship? As usual, he was high on *Yaba*[3] and was demanding money.

Fucking hell, John had already paid him 30,000 baht in advance, but somehow he was broke already. You know, I could swear that the cheap perfume from Yam was in the air but when I asked him, he just laughed and drew back on the spliff that we were sharing. He started pushing me and saying that I slept with hippos for money. I reminded him that the 'hippo' in question was paying him for his services - exactly what services, I didn't know.

---

3   *Yaba – literal translation 'Crazy Drug' is a potent amphetamine also known internationally as Ice. It's a mixture of methamphetamine and caffeine, by far the most popular drug in Thailand today and is often used by those in 'The Industry' to forget the lifestyle they are currently 'chained' to. Usually in a red tablet form, Yaba is crushed and heated up in foil. The user inhales this heady mixture with a straw and the 'hit' is almost immediate. Sadly, many lose their lives and/or freedom after the addiction is formed.*

In fact, John and Boi had been out for drinks the previous night, and it was my turn to be jealous. They hadn't come home until this morning and were acting as if they were the best of friends, not rivals for my affection. I slapped Boi as hard as I could, and even though his face went a bright pink, he just laughed and punched me right back. There was blood everywhere and I couldn't see a thing. When I finally stood up, he was gone. I then heard John calling me from upstairs so rushed to the bathroom to fix the damage before seeing what the hell he wanted.

Boi

So, I felt a little bad at punching Ying in the face, after all she has helped me so much and I can see some kind of future with her, so long as the money comes in a few years.

But I am a Thai man and no woman can tell me what to do. How dumb can she be?

I prefer making love to Yam who has a much better body, and her tits are natural, not hard plastic like Ying's. I even went out for a drink with the hippo last night and despite my expectations, it was not too bad at all. He smells and sweats like a stuck boar, but the man has money, and that is one quality that I respect above all else.

I'm moving Yam back to her village next week, when I'll be able to have as much of her sweet stuff that I can handle. Of course, I'll be here for Ying, but given the choice, I know which one I would prefer.

John seems a little bit weird though, and when we went into the Buriram gogo bars, he seemed to get excited when the young server girl was paying us attention. He asked in his ridiculous Thai if he could pay her to sit on his lap. Well, this is Thailand where everything is for sale. He looked ecstatic when the poor girl was bouncing around on his lap. I thought to tell Ying, but then I decided to keep this one as a secret for myself.

Who knows when I might need a favour from Old Hippo?

John

Well that was a surprise, who would have thought that Boi was such a resourceful guy. Ying must think I am a stupid idiot if she is trying to pass him off as her friend/brother/whatever.

Of course, he's screwing her and I couldn't care less.

To be honest, I only married her to live over in Thailand anyway. Sure, she's super-hot, but I prefer them way younger and preferably without any family to worry about. So, when I saw that teenager last night, I just knew that this was the right place for me to see out my days. I made enough money in the UK to live like a king here in Isaan and I will be far away from any prying eyes.

I'll keep stringing Ying along and play the White Buffalo just as long as I can. Boi seems to be a man with his own mind, so I will pay him what he wants, just so long as he keeps setting me up with sexy young things.

I'll never return to the UK as I know what's waiting for me there.

Yeah, just stay here and provide for Ying and do whatever the fuck I want.

What could possibly go wrong?

***

Ban Pon, Buriram Province

Yam

I wasn't surprised when I got the call to come up to Buriram Province from Boi last week. He can't get enough of my body and when I realised that he was up here with that plastic bitch Ying, it was impossible to refuse.

Boi has plans for us and he says I only have to wait for two years before he finishes with her for good. He'll take his share of their Buffalo winnings and take me away to live with him forever.

The only fly in this ointment is that I have been missing my periods, and that could make him think differently.

I'll keep the baby bump under wraps for now, because any decent Thai man would run a mile knowing that there's a child on the way.

Apart from that, Boi is the perfect man.

Well, as close to perfect as I will ever get…

***

On the road, Khon Kaen Province

Kwan

We took a day and a half to get back to the spot where we nearly ran over the blue-eyed beauty and booked into a cheap hotel for the night. It was a small town just outside of Nong Kai and we were close to the Laos border. Typically, Somluk had decided to have a few quiet drinks and an early night but I had other plans.

Some say I was addicted to three things: drugs, booze and sex.

They were correct. I had struggled with these demons ever since I was old enough to earn just about what I needed to pay for these vices. Thankfully, Isaan was a place where all three were readily available and cheap.

We had to share a room because the rest were taken, and I started thinking of ways to convince Somluk to lend me some baht because I was pretty much broke right now. He seemed a bit quiet, so I was really doing him a favour anyway.

Somluk

I had really been looking forward to a good night's sleep before the hard work started tomorrow but sharing a room with that little idiot meant that I had zero chance of this. He was a noisy bastard and snored loud enough to wake the dead. Of course, he wanted to go out for food and drinks and probably would insist on looking for the nearest brothel. There was no way of getting Kwan to change his mind so I resigned myself for yet another night of debauchery.

'Somluk, can you advance me a few thousand baht, please?'

I could hardly believe my ears. He still owed me ten big ones from the last mission, and I reminded him that we got a big fat zero for that waste of time.

We had a few beers and eventually, as always, I softened. Once we'd finished the Tom Yam Goong, we were heading for the Golden Eagle Club. It sounded posh, but it essentially was the cheapest knocking shop in the village. I sighed as we entered the seedy place and could almost smell the used condoms as an ugly looking *Mamasan*[4] shuffled over with the menu of available ladies. The prices were really low and I shuddered to think of the quality of flesh on offer as I turned to speak to Kwan.

But he was already upstairs.

Yes, it was going to be another long night as I looked at the drab goods on display... a real long night.

∗∗∗

Thepprasit Road, Jomtien, near Pattaya

Wannee

I spotted four attractive dark-skinned girls when the bus emptied and wasted no time in herding them over to our van. Each one had a good figure, big boobs and decent enough faces.

I could never understand why westerners liked this particular look, as Thai men would never pay for sex with these girls. The dark skin indicated poverty, as they had probably already spent years toiling under the fierce Isaan sun in the rice fields. But it was a consumer's market, and these were probably the easiest to deal with, the paler skinned girls from the Chiang Mai region were usually a bit stuck up and quicker to realise that they had some value.

They all ended up the same after all was said and done, doomed to work the bars of Pattaya until they were too old to earn money for the establishment, and then usually forced to scrap a living hanging

---

4   ***Mamasan*** – *Common name for a lady who runs the bar or club and is a more polite word for pimp in most cases. Usually these are ex-bar girls who are well past their sell by date and can be somewhat bossy and bitter to younger, more attractive bar workers.*

out on the Beach Road, trying to catch the eye of equally scummy sex tourists who were looking for a bargain lay.

As we pulled into the spacious driveway outside my house, I laughed inwardly at the excited chattering that was taking place at the back of my van.

Poor idiots seemed to think that this would be where they were going to live.

'Okay ladies, move your pretty little arses out of the van and let's get inside for some food and rest!'

They scurried out and into the house where I had laid on a relative Isaan feast for these pathetic excuses of humanity.

***

Ban Mee, Buriram Province

Ice

I was up very early today and decided to feed and water Dad's fighting cocks before he had even woke up. He would spend more time with these evil little monsters than our family, which is something Mum would often mention when we sat down for a meal. It was true though, the money coming into the house wasn't much, but most seemed to be wiped out when dad returned from a session of gambling and cock fighting every weekend.

Mum worked at the local factory for about fourteen hours a day making shoes. The salary wasn't much, and I could see the pain in her eyes when she noticed how the little money she'd make would be taken by Dad for his expensive habit.

Today was my first day at the 7-11, and I felt a tiny flutter in my stomach as I approached the shiny shop. It looked so out of place compared to the buildings on either side, and I *wai*-ed to the spirit house outside the double doors as I did my best to look calm. I was almost halfway through the entrance when I felt a tug on my arm.

It was Bank.

'Come here, *Nong-Sao*. I need to ask you a favour, please.'

38

He stunk of marijuana weed, and I could smell the whisky fresh on his breath.

This was why I hated Thai men so much, they seemed to have no idea of responsibility and even less clue about how to act in public. I pulled free and sprinted for the doors before they closed. I looked back, only to notice he had disappeared from sight.

As I turned my gaze, I was met by someone else.

'Welcome Ice, my name is Poon, and I am your manager.'

At least this one had manners.

I smiled sweetly and was immediately put to work, sweeping the already spotless floor.

Bank

That little bitch!

First, she lets me down by not showing enough respect to come to work with me on the second day, and now she's embarrassed me in public. I was going to give her a big surprise today, even had the condoms in my pocket, but that was going to have to wait.

Yesterday I snuck into her bedroom but had to go when my phone started ringing. It was my ex-wife, who had the cheek to ask me for money for our son. I was bored of that relationship years ago and wondered how I could just make her vanish into thin air. Thai woman are okay, but they are just so damn bossy and possessive. I had to remind her that she was the one who kicked me out three years earlier because I was 'sleeping around' - what did she expect? In Thailand, we men are the superior sex, and women are just there to keep us amused.

I had to move back home with Mum and, to be honest, that suited me. Dad had killed himself years ago, and Mum treated me like a little emperor.

Why couldn't all women be just like Mum? I smoked another joint and lay down for a sleep in my hammock at the back of the house.

As usual, my dreams were full of that little slut Ice, and I soon had my evil way with her.

She was even wearing that tight 7-11 uniform.

Nice touch…

***

Somchai

By the time I realised that Bot was trying to get me drunk, it was far too late.

He knew that I was jealous of his wealth and just kept pouring the expensive imported whisky down my throat. I didn't mind so much, but when he finally indicated that it was my turn to pay for the drinks, the scorn on his face was almost too much for me to take. I was just about to punch him in his big flat nose when he started laughing and just ordered more.

'You see, my old friend, you really should think about getting Ice into the entertainment business…'

That was the final straw for me.

'Listen Bot, I may not have your money, but at least my family has self-respect!'

I had fallen into his trap…

Bot

I guess it's true, you can't educate stupid.

Somchai was both poor and dumb, what a winning combination. The only thing he had that I had ever wanted was his wife – Patty. She was the most beautiful girl in the village, and I still yearned for her. It was so far unrequited, but I still held a torch for her.

It was true so far that money can't buy you everything, but I was still working on that. The closest I could get was to make her see what a waste her husband was. Of course, I'd never leave my wife, but surely, as one of the richest men in the village, she would open her legs for me now?

'Tell you what Somchai, how about a friendly wager?'

I started to see some light at the end of this 20-year tunnel.

'Let's put our best fighting cocks in a battle to the death.'

He mumbled something about not having the money right now, but I already had the perfect solution.

'If your rooster wins, I'll gladly pay you 100,000 baht…'

His greedy little eyes opened as wide as the Mekong River in Rainy Season.

'…but if mine manages to kill yours, you let me sleep with your wife.'

I just managed to get that last word out before the old cripple smashed a full bottle of Johnny Walker Black over my head, and the lights went out.

***

Ying

I really thought that the bad days were over.

Boi hadn't punched me like this since we left Pattaya last month.

The makeup covered up the bruise, but I was still in utter agony inside. John didn't notice, and I doubted he would give a shit even if he did. I knew that Thai men were complicated compared to foreigners, but why did they have to hit so fucking hard?

I knew Boi loved me and I still loved him, but I started to doubt the whole relationship after this last beating. Every Thai man I had laid down with ended up using me as a beautiful punch bag and, after a few dozen thrashings, I would end the relationship.

But Boi was different to them.

I was sure of it.

Yet how come the scent of that bitch Yam always crept up my nostrils every time I held him close?

Boi

I had a feeling that Ying was suspecting something, she seemed to

41

have a troubled expression on her face when we were close. Surely she wasn't a mind reader?

Then I realised, it was Yam's perfume!

She used to spray it on me after we had made love, and I guess it was such a unique scent that Ying was subconsciously associating it to Yam. I made a note to tell her to change her cologne and started the motorbike up.

I was looking forward to a good night out for a change.

But it wasn't Ying riding pillion, neither was it Yam.

No, I was going out for night of debauchery with a human being who weighed more than the three of us combined!

John

I noticed that Ying was wearing twice as much makeup as usual and guessed that Boi had been hitting her.

I couldn't really give a shit to be honest, but also I didn't fancy any unwanted attention right now. The Thai Police were a useless bunch but even so, I needed to stay clear of their radar for now, because I couldn't bear the thought of being told to leave Thailand.

As Boi pulled the bike over to the large building next to Buriram Bus Station, I felt that familiar twitching in my loins once more.

We were finally at the Tawen Daeng, and I really hoped that his description of this bawdy place was no exaggeration.

✳✳✳

Ban Pon, Buriram Province

Yam

I was in tears when Boi cancelled our date at the last minute, especially as I suspected he was going to spending our time with that slut Ying! I understood my place in this relationship, but that didn't mean that I was happy to share him.

Not at all.

But he swore that he was just going out with the obese Englishman married to Ying and promised to make time for me when he returned.

The plan for us to be finally together had started to crumble and I was even more insecure than when we used to see each other back in Pattaya. We'd snatch a moment here and there, and I was always aware that I was number 2 when it came to having dibs on this beautiful man.

I waited until 3 am, but when it was clear that my bed was going to remain empty, I called the local dealer and decided to invest in a few hits of Yaba instead.

The night was ruined, but at least I could get some solace in this hazy state of mind.

✳✳✳

Ban Mee, Buriram Province

Patty

I had long since feared that this family was doomed and I was under no illusion that Somchai was the main protagonist.

He was a lovely man right up until that work accident. I accepted that his leg would never mend, however the real damage was not so easy to deal with. It was if his soul had been torn out of his very being, and we were left with a stranger, an angry man who was unrecognisable, and certainly not the man I had once fallen deeply in love with.

Despite working my heart out at that dreary factory, he was never grateful, and our shared secret would eventually need to be revealed.

It was obvious that we had to remove Ice from her school if we had a chance to hang onto our home. Months behind on the rent and with no sign of my husband getting a meaningful job, we had no choice. I had asked for more hours at the shoe factory, but I doubted that my body could stand up to more than fourteen-hour shifts.

Ice had started work at the local 7-11 and although that would help, I knew that there was only one way for her to really help this family. When I noticed that Ying had passed our house a few times, this was a stark reminder to me.

Somchai was typically stubborn about this decision that I had already made, no surprise there really.

I wept inside but was already counting the days until she realised that her future was already mapped out.

Ice needed to follow in Ying's footsteps and start looking for a job in The Industry as a sex worker…

***

Khon Kaen Province

Somluk

'Open the door or we will smash it down!'

Hardly the way I like to start my mornings, but this sounded urgent and I stumbled to the door, head and belly full of cheap alcohol as the Police pushed past me. I counted about four or maybe five of these busy little bastards, and as they pinned me to the wall, I started to realise that my daft colleague had, yet again, upset the locals.

'Where is Kwan?'

Yes, I was right as always, the useless bastard was to blame for me losing the right to a much-needed lie-in. He'd pay for this in more ways than one.

After a few minutes of intense shouting that was making my hangover even worse, it was apparent that Kwan had caused quite the problem last night. I tried to recollect my thoughts as they brought me up to date. Once I'd paid for the meagre services from last night, I had found a liquor store and splashed out a few hundred baht on a bottle of Mekong rum.

As for Kwan, well, he had different plans.

According to the Boys in Brown, Kwan had scored some tablets from the local dealer and then had tried his best to paint the shitty little town red.

Indeed, there were reports of a short and slight man raising merry hell once last orders had been called in the bus station restaurant. For me this was just about the last straw, because I had told him countless times that when we are working, no drugs are to be used.

After they left, I had a few more hours sleep before packing up and hitting the road. I just couldn't be bothered to waste any more time looking for this degenerate colleague of mine.

Maybe the consequences that he was going to have to deal with would shake him up enough to seek a different path.

Just maybe…

Kwan

This time I knew that I had really screwed up, why couldn't I be more like Somluk?

I woke up in some strange car that I had stolen last night, and by the way the seatbelt was biting into my stomach, I was upside down. As I pressed the button, my entire body smashed into the vehicle's roof and I blacked out for a few minutes. My head was aching and there was water everywhere.

I couldn't work out where I was, but the fact I had bothered to fastened the seatbelt annoyed me even more.

Crawling out of the wreck, I clawed my way out of the ditch and looked into the midday sun. My phone was gone, and I had no idea where I was or what time it was.

All I knew was that I had really screwed up.

'Put your hands behind your head!'

Those were the last words I heard as a dull blow struck me just behind the ear and I lost consciousness.

***

Thepprasit Road, Jomtien, near Pattaya

Wannee

I hadn't heard from the two goons so far and that could mean one of two things: either they were hard at work, or one of them, probably Kwan, had been locked up again.

I accepted that it was probably the latter and walked to the lounge where the four trainee whores were still fast asleep.

'Wake up you little bitches, today is the first day of the rest of your life!'

I smirked as one by one, the farm girls stretched and looked around in confusion as they realised that, also present in the room, were a dozen men, all looking on with desire and evil thoughts.

Long ago I had developed a plan that not only worked well but would, in an odd way, teach these girls how The Industry actually worked. So far, the success rate for my bitches was around eighty percent.

Breaking these figures down in a way that made me happy, was a little like this: 80 percent of my whores would not only survive their first and most profitable year – but they would possibly thrive in this new seedy environment and continue for a few more years to bring money to me and my six bars. As for the remaining twenty percent, they would not.

I owned six bars here in Pattaya at various locations and two Karaoke bars plus a few brothels in Cambodia. Typically, the girls would be moved between these venues at my discretion. I would provide lodgings and food for the first three months. During this time, the girls had no salary whatsoever.

If this seems harsh, it's for their own good.

This period of time would weed out the pondlife that were simply not built for this lifestyle. These losers would meet an untimely end either at their own hands or by mine. After all, they couldn't go back home after failing at the world's oldest profession.

What else could they do?

No, I was simply accelerating their karma and ridding the country of low-hanging fruit that had already left the tree and festered to the core.

So back to their training, I looked on, whisky in hand as the waiting men chose their collective favourite and continued to enjoy the show as the one-way orgy started.

***

Ban Mee, Buriram Province

Ice

With my first day at work completed, I walked home thinking of my life ahead There was no way that I could continue living in this village, I was sure of that by now. I grimaced at the alternative options but knew inside me that I had to leave my family home if I was to ever have a chance at happiness. The staff at 7-11 were nice people, but most were at University and were merely making a few extra baht to cover expenses, so I did not think I could easily create friendships with them.

That incident with Bank was worrying, and his reputation signalled that he had bad intentions for me. My thoughts wandered a little until they arrived at destination Ying.

Okay, she seemed to have money to burn, but at what cost?

Was I destined to spend the next ten years on my back turning tricks for foreign men?

I was just seventeen, and instead of looking forward to another three or possibly eight years of education, the bleak horizon made me shudder to the core.

I was always a resourceful girl, so instead of resigning myself to this tawdry fate, I started to do what I did best.

Thinking about the text my older friend Nok had recently sent me, I began to develop a plan.

Bank

I had slept through most of the day and lit a Marlboro just as Ice was walking past my house. I didn't waste any energy on this precocious cow because I had already given up on the nice approach.

47

Some people need to be told what to do, as freewill is a very expensive commodity these days. She would be mine, whatever she thought she was going to do.

I just needed to work out the most obvious route. Chuckling for no apparent reason, I tabbed through at my list of phone contacts and stopped on one particular name.

It read 'Somluk'...

***

Somchai

Bot had overstepped the mark this time, and as I walked away from his prone body, I glanced back to see blood running freely from the fresh wound, visible through his thick, greasy hair.

He was now a rich man and I was at the mercy of people of influence, what would he do once he came around?

I always had a hot temper and was a fiercely jealous man, especially where my wife was concerned.

Ying

I was ready to kill somebody when I realised that John and Boi were out again. What the hell was going on?

I was the one who decided where these relationships were going, except now it seemed that I was on the back seat instead of steering my way to a better future. I decided to visit the village bar and took a seat outside. Apparently, Dad and Somchai had been in a fight earlier, but I had no interest in that. Bank was there and, again, not interested in that pathetic loser either, especially when he started talking about that kid, Ice. I knew Thai men like them young, but this was pushing it, even for him.

I knocked back a few gin and tonics, and though the content of the spirit had started to cloud my senses, I saw something unmistakeable that nearly knocked me off my stool.

A motorcycle passed the bar very slowly and when I looked up, there was absolutely no doubt the rider was that very bitch who was trying to get her claws into my man.

Made up to the nines and wearing next to nothing, staring right at me with a mixture of mirth and pure hatred, it could only be one whore.

Yes, it was Yam!

Boi

I was usually spot on when it came to understanding people on first appearance, but John was actually far more interesting than I had estimated. Yes, he was a fat smelly foreign bastard, that much could not be denied, but underneath, well this was a different matter entirely.

He was rich, which wasn't something that he hid, but he was also crafty, sneaky and very greedy. These were three of my favourite qualities!

Tomorrow was the first day of *Songkran*,[5] the Thai New Year, and John was throwing a party for the whole village.

But this wasn't just another show of wealth, not at all. He knew how to influence people and win friends, and this seemed to be just the start of his next move.

I glanced over and the ridiculous looking man had at least four underage girls clawing him for food and attention. He seemed to know exactly how to keep them coming back.

We exchanged looks and I started to think that he was the one to listen to, not that stupid bitch Ying.

---

5   ***Songkran*** – *Thai Buddhist New Year, usually on the 13th of April. Plenty of celebrations typically consisting of water-throwing and drinking. It is a time of celebration in Thailand, and even the poorest villages would put their lives on hold as communities would enjoy the activity of throwing water over each other. The whole festival was based on cleaning out last year's sins and mistakes and starting over again. In some parts of Thailand, Pattaya and Chiang Mai, it would carry on for a week and buckets of ice would be hurled into the paths of motorcyclists and result in thousands of accidents and no small amount of deaths. The death toll is as hideous as the feeling of being hit in the face with solid ice from aforementioned buckets.*

John

This was more like it! Christ, these girls were younger than any I had seen down in Pattaya, Boi sure was living up to his reputation as a bad boy.

I was throwing a massive Thai New year party tomorrow and he was helping with the arrangements. I wanted to meet everyone in the village and had invited a few big wigs from Buriram city as well.

I needed to get the Police boys on my side as I had plans of my own for some kind of club in the future. This would be off the radar, but open to a select group of people with - how shall I put this - the same eclectic tastes as yours truly. Instead of putting more thought into the party, I decided to change tack and brought forward my plans for Cambodia by some months.

I felt as if I didn't act soon, things good go South with Ying and I needed her to stay sweet at least until I left Thailand.

It would be the perfect decoy and I discussed this with Boi in some detail.

To my surprise, he had no loyalty to his girl and had a greed, like mine, that he was starting to realise that only I could feed.

Now, if only I could keep that boring cow Ying occupied in the meantime…

Yam

I awoke with a crushing headache, the ones that only Yaba can cause, and spent the rest of the afternoon just moping around the house. Eventually, Mum told me to get out, so I took the old motorbike and started riding around the village.

I had a feeling in my loins that only one man could satisfy and he was so close that I could almost taste his sweet tongue in my soaking wet pussy.

Although he had forbade me to ever visit him in his village, I was so damn horny that I risked the hideous temper that had bruised my body many times.

The fact was that Thai men only hit their women when they were really in love with them and I wore those bruises and a couple of scars as badges of honour.

Sure I had a few farang customers who begged me to come and live in their countries but the idea made me want to vomit.

Making love to Boi was on a different level and after sex, they would want to cuddle me as if I was their fucking mother and not the woman who was faking the orgasms like a Hollywood actor.

In contrast, Boi would light up a cigarette, offer me one if he felt I deserved it. and then go out for a few beers with his friends like the real man he was.

So I did a few circuits of our shit hole village and imagined it was me and not Ying who was most probably being fucked by him at this moment.

Eventually my horniness and the fact I was carrying his baby just got the better of him.

Yes it was time to tell him he would be the father of our child.

I had already chosen a name.

Boon Mee.

This meant good luck and for sure, this little angel would have a very special life, unlike his unremarkable mother.

I decided to pop over to the next village, where Boi and his whore were living.

It was only 20 minutes on my fast little bike and I found the monstrous new house easily. In fact, I could see it from about a mile away, as it looked so ridiculous compared to the wooden buildings that made up most of the villagers' homes.

There seemed to be nobody there, and I thought about smashing a few windows until I noticed that some of the lights upstairs were on. I decided a better use of my time and energy would be having a quick tour of the village instead.

It was almost identical to my own apart from the western house. Eventually, I decided to go back home and called my dealer for some more Yaba.

That was when I noticed her.

Sat outside the local bar, as bright as brass - it was Ying!

Just like the vulgar house she lived in; this whore didn't fit in with her surroundings anymore.

Dressed like the Soi 6 slut she was, Ying was knocking back the booze alone outside the bar.

I drove past at least three times and looked her straight in the eye on every pass.

On the final drive by, she was looking back at me with scorching hatred behind her dilated pupils. I met her gaze right back, imagining her to be an Asian water monitor just about to be flattened by an eighteen-wheeler.

***

Thai New Year's Day - Songkran

Patty

As I saw the sun rise through the holes in our roof, I looked over to see Somchai sprawled across the wooden floor. Today was the first day of *Songkran*, the Thai New year.

Traditionally, this was a time for celebration, throwing out old for new. But I had a feeling of dread this time around. Nothing was going well and we, as a family, seemed to be heading rapidly into a downward spiral.

I gave my husband a kick in the stomach as I walked past him. To my surprise, he opened those bloodshot eyes and gave me a confused look, which quickly turned into excitement.

'Happy Songkran darling, I have some great news for us!'

Somchai seemed almost delirious with happiness.

'Oh really, why is that?' I shot back with sarcasm.

'We have come into money, in fact 100,000 baht. It is enough for us to have a new start! We can even move out of this shitty house.'

'I spoke to Bot last night', he went on.

This aroused my interest and was just about to ask for more details when he hit me with the killer blow:

'All you have to do is sleep with him, just for one night'…

End of Chapter Two

CHAPTER THREE — ALL MESSED UP

Khon Kaen Province

Kwan

I awoke in the police cell with the familiar crashing sounds of Songkran in my mind. It was as if I had my own private orchestra creating a hideous cacophony in the recesses of my mangled mind.

This was my 45th year on Earth, and for some time I had realised that my time here would not be long. Strangely, I thought back to my youth and the memories of growing up. I suppose they were no different to most other poor families. We never had enough money for food, and when I developed my drug addiction, that only added to my personal agony. Dad was no better, except his vice was legal, and he would often steal any money from the family noodle jar only to pour the cheap liquor down his throat.

I used to wonder why he stayed with Mum for so long, because her complaining was enough to wake the dead from at least three generations.

By the time I realised that she was the only reason we managed to stay together as a family, well, it was too late. My sister Nong had long since fled and, according to distant friends and relatives, she sold her body in Phuket for enough for a fix of whatever she could get her hands on.

I often wondered how such a pitiful collection of souls could exist?

Mum would offer food and gifts to the monks every time they walked past the house, and I could see the pity in their eyes.

The last few years working for the CFC only compounded my realisation that I would soon be escaping from this particular wheel of *Samsara.*[1]

I suppose the near escape with that blasted crocodile was the final act of my wasted life. I knew that Somluk would be okay, so long as he found that blue-eyed bitch, but ultimately, he would also eventually be replaced by that vicious whore Wannee.

As I secured my leather belt around the bars on the window and around my neck, I thought about what lay ahead, but I knew that if I were reborn, it would be as a cockroach because I was worth nothing more, or even less.

Somluk

I had a gut-wrenching feeling that Kwan was now gone, I had carried him for more than a decade, and my only chance of redemption now was to find the blue-eyed beauty. On the way to that shitty village, I decided I should stop by and see my old buddy Bank.

He had sent me a garbled message about a young local girl that he believed had at least some potential.

The photo looked good and I felt that I could snag her on the way back to Pattaya after grabbing the prize up North.

***

Thepprasit Road, Jomtien, near Pattaya

Wannee

Out of the group of girls who I had chosen, one had caught my eye. Her name was Preem, and she was very pretty indeed. Although I enjoyed sex with men, I had a thing for girls who looked a little submissive, and Preem certainly ticked all of the boxes.

As a younger woman, I spent a lot of baht on plastic surgery. My nose, cheeks and breasts were transformed beyond recognition. But

---

1   **Samsara** – *Part of Buddhist beliefs that we are constantly revolving in a circle known as the Wheel of Samsara. Karma and fate are part of this cycle of life and reincarnation.*

as the years passed me by, the once youthful features started to fade and sag. Mother nature was indeed cruel and these days, I had to pay for sex if I wanted an attractive buck. Even more if I wanted to fuck a female. So, my only real pleasure was to pick one of the farm fresh girls, and tonight, Preem was the one.

I had long since given up on meeting a man, Thai or foreign, that could be my equal. They were so dull and predictable, and the only men who would look at me twice were despicable, usually bald and fat and with less personality than my faithful Samart.

So, I led Preem to my room and imagined that as I tasted her youthful juices, at least for fifteen minutes, I was young again and hadn't ruined my once youthful features beyond recognition.

***

Ban Mee, Buriram Province

Ice

I awoke to the sound of the village pickup blaring traditional Thai music well before 6 in the morning. My mind was absolutely mashed thanks to the last few days.

I had been relegated from the oldest child in the family trying to make something of herself, to one of the breadwinners. The fact that I was starting to harbour sexual feelings towards any decent looking man only added to this funky outlook on life. As I walked to work, I did a mental check on the potential men that would probably, eventually, take my precious virginity.

Number one on the probability list was Bank, more due to conjuncture than my wants. He was decent looking, but way too old. There were a few boys at school that were interested, but I seriously doubted that they would have a clue. The main problem was that whoever got to first place would end up being my husband. That was just the way it was here in rural Thailand.

I would marvel over the girls in my favourite magazine who had their pick of men. I just knew that I would end up with some abusive bastard who didn't even look good.

59

As I arrived at 7-11, I got absolutely soaked by the assistant manager.

'*Sawasdee Pee Mai!*' he yelled in my direction; this was the traditional Thai Happy New Year salutation that allowed the water thrower to get away with the inevitable punishment that would be coming.

He hurled a bucket of ice-cold water over me outside the sliding doors and afterwards seemed to be staring at my chest a little too long.

He was alright to look at, but I knew he was bisexual, and that really didn't feature in my future plans.

I started to stack the shelves, thinking about my family, and felt more than a little bitter about the fact I had now become an adult, at least a few years earlier than planned.

Apparently, we could leave early today, but with no extra pay.

I had a feeling in my gut that this Songkran would change my life forever.

Boi

I was feeling a bit mixed up this morning, not because of the stupid bitches that were eventually going to fight over me, that happened every year - no, I was thinking more about what John had offered me. Even though I was no pervert, the money he offered me to set up a new place over in Cambodia was just too much to ignore.

Of course, I was worried about the police and the attention that could occur, but I was more excited about the massive lump sum he was dangling in front of me.

I hated perverts, and John was certainly one of the worst I had met. He made no secret of his desires and I almost pitied Ying. But she was a big girl and could easily snag another lonely Westerner if needed.

I didn't have many standards and I lived my life to the full, so decided to chat to him when we met later in the day.

Bank

Life was dull and seemed to be getting worse. As a Thai man I usually felt that I was blessed and typically opportunities would just fall into my lap but this year, well that wasn't the case. The call from Somluk was a small bonus but I seriously doubted that I could encourage Ice to play ball.

Girls these days were different and as I grew older, it was harder to get their interest. I looked at Ying who seemed to have it all, but I was the one who had put her on the road to riches, so who was to say I couldn't do it one more time with Ice?

I was meeting Somluk in a few hours to take advantage of my last chance before I eventually followed the dozens of girls down to Bangkok, Pattaya, Phuket or wherever and sold my own arse for whatever I could get.

Life sucked, and it slowly dawned on me that I needed to get a reality check before my own looks faded.

Somluk had replied to my text and offered me a temporary way out of this mess.

It had been a while and I felt a little excitement as I told him to meet me outside the 7-11 later that day.

✱✱✱

Somchai

So today was yet another Songkran but this one would be different, I could feel it in my bones.

I was trying to convince my wife to sleep with my neighbour, but what could I do? He was so rich and certainly wanted Patty. The hundred thousand baht would pay off my gambling debts and leave me enough to start afresh. I love her, still but had to face facts.

I was into my fifties and had zero prospects. My daughters were going to cost me more money once they got married, and eventually I would be an old cripple and may as well be tossed in the garbage.

But I knew that Bot still lusted after my wife and needed to play that card immediately. I still loved her, but we were financially on the bones of our arses now. At the very least, I could do my best to make this happen.

Surely Patty could see that I was only doing what every other Thai man would do in my situation?

Every fucking year we tried to wipe away the sins of the previous 365 days, but we keep on making the same mistakes. My head hurt like hell, and I decided to make a strong coffee and try to clear my thoughts.

I was thinking about how to make amends to Bot for the beating I had delivered last night and, more importantly, how to get as much baht out of him for sleeping with Patty as possible.

Surely Patty could see that this tiny sacrifice was worth the effort? It wasn't as if I was asking her to be a whore.

If it were the other way round I would jump at the chance of having sex with another woman and wouldn't be so precious and selfish as to deny my family this windfall.

Maybe that was because I loved my wife and my kids, I would make the sacrifice.

I'd already broken the news to her earlier and would need to work on her as well. I sat on one of the plastic stools at the front of the house and as I looked up I realised, way too late, that the approaching pickup truck had at least ten standing passengers in the back that were about to unleash gallons of water my way.

There was little point in moving so I just shielded my cup with my hand to avoid the hassle of having to make another cup.

Just before they were on me, I heard a motorcycle coming the other way and looked up to see the truck smash into it head on.[2]

The poor girl must have been dead in seconds, as the truck seemed to engulf the bike and trample it into the tarmac before managing to stop. I half cursed this tragic event, knowing it would be the first of many over the next few days.

Days later, the incarcerated truck driver would be released after paying a small fine as he was directly related to the Poo yay Bahn, headman of our village.

It was also recorded that the lady driving the motorbike was not paying the slightest bit of attention and was more interested in texting her boyfriend.

Bot

Although that attack last night left me with a decent sized cut, most of it was covered by my thick hair. No stitches needed, and it would most probably heal in a few weeks – good thing that was, since I hated hospitals.

I started to develop a plan that would let me take Somchai's wife for a pittance. I was friends with most of the village police and even had a connection with Buriram's governor thanks to my recent wealthy status, and a few choice donations towards his slush fund. After Somchai had fled, I asked the barman to take a few photos for future insurance. Amazingly, he'd taken one of the actual attack, and it was clear enough to capture Somchai's features. Very resourceful young man he was, and I slipped him a few thousand baht for his troubles.

I needed an extra few hours of rest as I wasn't getting any younger, so by the time I arose, the sun was out in all of its glory and the

---

2   *Road traffic accidents - It's not commonly known, but Thailand has one of the highest rates of road traffic accidents in the world. Almost always in the top 5 and only a few third-world countries in Africa have a worse record. When you consider the fact that Thailand is seen as a top tourist destination only compounds the levity of this tragic fact. Typically, there will be around 60 deaths every single day and these are a mixture of drivers, passengers and hapless pedestrians who meet their maker(s). During Songkran, this number is tripled, if not quadrupled. The water throwing by the roadside certainly doesn't help and the intoxication of the drivers only adds to Thailand's inclusion in this hideous hall of fame.*

temperature was as high as I could remember.

Usually I couldn't stand Songkran, but this year was different. I marvelled at how my fortunes had changed and just laughed as the passing kids emptied their water buckets over my sore head. I'd probably need a few injections to deal with potential infection from the dirty contents but right now, I really did not care.

'*Sawasdee Pee Mai!*' I returned with some gusto as the cheeky little scamps refilled their water pistols and buckets from my rain butt.

Ying

It had been years since I could get excited about Songkran, in my opinion the idea of washing away the sins was a pile of shit because we make our own luck in this world.

Even in my early teens, I would look at the life my Mother had worked so hard for and decided I would take a different path. She was the most religious woman I knew, and the only reason she was able to enjoy her life was because of the hours I had endured on my back down in Pattaya. Although she never really spoke of my job, I knew that she appreciated the good fortune that I had bestowed on my family.

She could scarcely look John in the eye, but she knew that he was the best thing that could have happened. I no longer had to pretend to be nice to ugly foreign strangers, and in a few years' time, she would look back and laugh about it all. I fully intended to start a new family with Boi and maybe then, her and Dad would come and join us in the new house.

There was, however, a huge fly in that particular ointment, and I decided that today would be a good time to get that pesky insect finally swatted into oblivion. I would have a serious discussion with John and try to convince him to accelerate our visa application for the UK and do my best to ensure that the slut threatening to take my man was removed from the situation once and for all.

The party at our house was going to bring a lot of important people into John's life, yet he seemed almost nonchalant about the whole event. Weirdly, he could talk of nothing else up until that evening he had spent with Boi -something had changed, and I needed to find out what that was.

After showering I dried myself and chose the sexiest underwear possible in order to make John realise what he had to lose if he didn't get his act together.

***

Yam

Listening to the traditional Thai music blaring from the passing water truck, I awoke from my dreams knowing I had to move fast if I had a chance of getting my life back on track.

I hadn't seen Boi for a few days and this meant that he'd lost interest in my charms. The look and demeanour I noticed on the face and body language of my love rival last night also indicated that she too was becoming detached from his affections. I guessed that the fat foreigner had something to do with this, and mentally racked my brains for some clues.

Avoiding breakfast as I knew my pregnancy was starting to show, I showered and dressed in my tightest shorts and sexiest top before kicking my motorbike into life.

I was heading for a showdown today and had made up my mind that this New Year's Day would finally be the one that I deserved.

I reached the next village without getting a soaking, although I had to swerve a few times as the kids and a few adults aimed their oversized water pistols in my direction on the road linking the two places.

Still unsure of my game plan, as I rode into my target destination, I could feel my phone start to vibrate. I hoped that this was my lover and imagined that it would be the good news that I prayed for, that he finally had made up his mind about our relationship.

Without slowing down, I prepared myself for the news that would shape the future of my and our unborn child.

I deftly used one hand to open up the new message, as some of the commotion ahead made its way to my ears.

Looking up, I cursed my luck as I saw death approaching in the shape of a pickup truck only metres away.

Instead of trying desperately to steer away from this collision, I had enough time to open the message to read the meagre contents.

'We are finished!'

My mind registered this harsh directive instantly as I then ploughed straight into the oncoming vehicle. It engulfed me and my bike as if we were but a fly in its path. There was nothing left for me and it was simply an opportunity to finish my suffering once and for all.

I resigned myself and the life of my baby to whatever fate Buddha had planned for us in our next lives, on this most celebrated of days.

John

I had planned my next move with Boi and we agreed that Songkran would provide enough of a distraction for us to leave the village and our shared partner forever.

Okay, I had wasted a few quid on this house and the vehicles for Ying's family, but that was peanuts compared to my savings. I counted myself as one of the brightest people on the planet thanks to my heavy investment in Bitcoin a few years earlier. Although I had withdrawn over half of the profits, some £20 million pounds, the remaining half had already tripled that amount. I was obscenely rich and had serious plans for the future that didn't include Ying, her leeching family and this ridiculous shitty little village.

But thanks to those bastard charges against me back in the UK for possession of images and a few half-baked profiling accusations, I needed to make as little fuss as possible to curb any dramatics that may lead to my profile being looked into, and I had to make sure that Ying didn't kick off.

The Thai women that I had met so far had all been complete head-cases and when they got upset, as she was bound to, it wouldn't be long before a massive scene would ensue. Even the New Year celebrations could not hold a candle to a Thai woman who has been scorned, betrayed and whatever else her crazy mind wanted to add to that list of disrespectful outcomes.

Tonight's party was just a sham, as I realised I would be over the border and heading towards Sihanoukville long before they realised that I was gone.

Boi texted me and he'd already told his second lover that things had ended between them. As I heard Ying knock on the bedroom door and slowly opened it with hardly any clothes on, I inwardly sighed and steeled myself for what was going to happen next.

Patty

After hearing the indecent proposal from Somchai about the money for sleeping with Bot, I washed and dressed, kissed my two youngest daughters goodbye and took our creaky motorcycle out for a ride. It was clear that my marriage was now over, but I really needed to work out what was best for my daughters.

I knew Ice would be okay, she was smart and pretty, and would no doubt find a man soon enough. I could only hope that he would not be cut from the same cloth as the man I had married.

My own mother had told me that Somchai wasn't right for me even before I had broken the news to her. She had heard tales of his brash ways and despite this, she knew that I had little choice.

The tears streamed from my eyes as I revisited the memories from that distant place in time. I had filed the whole series of events deep into my brain and heart, and seldom had the courage to open that door into my soul I had tried to keep shut for so long.

I fell in love with Jet the minute I saw him.

His family had recently moved into town, and although he was three or four years older than me, he looked young enough to still be at school. Jet had a certain way about him that made my nether regions tremble like never before.

I had learned that he was from the *On Nut*[3] district in Bangkok, his

---

3   **On Nut** – *A district of Bangkok where a famous statue dedicated to Mae Nak was built to honour her existence. Many Thais visit the statue and indeed pray to Mae Nak to help them to win the lottery!*

family were forced to move to our village for reasons unknown, but I thanked my lucky stars that he was here and seemed to be very interested in me!

They moved into the empty house over the road and I found myself making excuses to visit his sister who was in my class at school.

It didn't take long before we became an item and were inseparable from then on. His knowledge of the world and the sexy Bangkok accent he carried so well made me hate every second that we were apart.

The summer afternoon where he turned me into a real woman was indeed the best and most tender moment of my life.

When I compare the clumsy fumbling of Somchai with Jet's gentle yet masculine technique, I still shudder and struggle to clear my mind.

We had plans to announce our engagement a few weeks later, but that was cut cruelly short by one fateful day.

It was the annual *conscription*[4] day, and it hadn't even dawned on me that my lover was to be involved in this event. It was kind of like the reverse of the Thai lottery, instead of having the lucky ticket that could lead to millions of baht, the fate of the winner/loser here would mean two years in the Thai army.

I will never forget the bemused look on Jet's handsome face as he revealed the colour of the ball he had fished out of the large wooden box.

It was red.

I sunk to the ground realising that this meant he would be taken away from me for two years. His family physically pulled him away from the rest of the young men who were lined up to learn and hopefully avoid Jet's fate.

Less than a month later we waved him off as Jet, son, brother and

---

4   **Conscription** – *When a Thai male reaches the age of 20, they must attend a ceremony that involves a bizarre game of chance. The would be 'conscriptees' place their hand into a bucket containing black and red balls, if they are unfortunate enough to pull out a red ball are required to join for a minimum of two years, black ball means you are free to leave.*

lover, climbed onto the army bus and out of our lives.

I moved in with his family and became very close to his mother, Kit.

We would spend a lot of time together and it was then that she spoke of *Mae Nak*.[5]

Legend has it that *Mae Nak Phra Khanong* was a beautiful girl from a farming family in Bangkok who fell in love with a handsome man named Mak, who, like my Jet, was conscripted into the army. But Mak was thrown directly into the war with the Shan tribe on the Burmese border. This was some 100 plus years ago, when we were at war with that country, and the fighting was brutal and many deaths were resulting on both sides.

Mae Nak fell pregnant with Mak's child as a result of their last night together. Tragically, both mother and child perished during a difficult childbirth. Mak, upon discharge, had heard nothing of this shattering event and when he returns, he is overjoyed to find both Mae Nak and their daughter waiting for him.

Eventually he discovers that his beloved wife and daughter are actually ghosts, and he flees for his life. Mae Nak chases her living husband and folklore has it that she caused havoc when was unable to find him.

At this point I would tune out from the rest of the details because I wasn't that interested at the time, as ghosts and religion didn't spike my curiosity as much as current events and love story magazines.

It was only many years later that I understood the reason for this 'history' lesson. She was warning me of what could lay ahead - did she know I was carrying her unborn grandchild even before I had?

Less than a month after we had waved brave Jet off, the entire household, myself, Kit and her husband, were rudely awakened by

---

5   **Mae Nak** – *Thais are deeply religious and also superstitious. The legend of Mae Nak involves a couple in love based over one hundred years ago. The man is drafted into the Thai Army leaving his pregnant wife. She later dies during childbirth and her returns. Mae Nak, the lady, appears to be alive and well with a healthy baby. It is only after some time he realises that both her and his son are in fact Ghosts! Mae Nak then pursues that hapless Mak, terrorising hm and anybody unlucky enough to help him.*

several firm knocks on the wooden front door.

I decided to turn back over and get some more sleep as for some reason, I was starting to fall into the habit of vomiting for no apparent reason, particularly in the mornings.

As I started to drift away, I started to try and make sense of the awful noises that were coming from downstairs.

'No, not Jet, not my only son!'

I sat bolt upright and threw on a few items of clothes before leaping out of bed, already shivering at the prospect of what had caused Kit to start wailing.

She was on her knees, and through the open door I could see the two uniformed men climb into their jeep and drive away.

I instinctively hugged Kit and no words were needed.

She was still holding the letterheaded document explaining how, just one month into his service, Jet had been blown apart by a Shan landmine.

The next few weeks were a blur as the funeral was held back in Bangkok where most of his friends and relatives resided. Although I was invited, I couldn't deal with reality just yet, and remained in Jet's house in the village.

I never saw Jet's family again, as it became clear that they were not coming back.

One month after returning to my own parents' house, I awoke one morning feeling desperately ill and less than an hour later, I was told by a pimply faced young doctor that I was in the second trimester of pregnancy.

I was carrying Ice, Jet's flesh and blood, and this provided the strength that I needed to continue with my life, whatever that had in store for me.

With these thoughts in my head, I parked the motorbike and got the key to the only available room, showered and waited for Bot.

On the road, somewhere near Buriram

Somluk

I got Bank's text on my way to the North East so took a slight detour towards the direction of Cambodia. As I drove past Buriram city and through the dozens of identical shithole villages, I marvelled at how people could live here. I myself was from a similar level of existence but had long since waved goodbye to the drudgery and tedium that were commonplace here in Isaan.

Songkran was in full flow and my truck was soon covered in the white mess that happens when talcum powder and water are mixed.

Bank was at the agreed destination, just outside a 7-11, and I pulled up near the entrance because he wanted to show me one of the girls he thought had potential. I was parched, so grabbed a few M150 energy drinks for the rest of the trip and noticed with some disgust that he was already three sheets to the wind.

I'd had enough of working with guys who were rarely sober but decided to let it slide for now. Kwan was probably still locked up, and I really didn't care to have to deal with yet another piss-head.

'There she is.'

Bank was pointing to the shop's server and, for once, he was bang on the money.

This girl, around seventeen I guessed, was beautiful and cheeky at the same time.

She looked over, shot a contemptuous frown at Bank, and went back to serving her customer with a drop-dead smile. Of course, she wasn't interested in an old fart like me, but that wasn't the point.

I made a mental note of her name tag, Ice, and filed her gorgeous face away for the next time I was passing through this dump of a place.

Soon we were miles away and Bank was fast asleep in the passenger seat.

Now I had one thing on my mind - she had blue eyes and a multimillion-baht price tag on her perfect face.

***

Ban Mee, Buriram Province

Ying

'Honey, why you no *boom boom*[6] me anymore?'

I leaned over to show my husband the paid-for breasts that he used to salivate over, but he looked disinterested, as if I were some old hag on Pattaya Beach Road who couldn't even give it away. As usual, he was on his iPad and already drinking whiskey. He had a spare glass next to him on the bedside table and offered it to me. Usually I would tell him to fuck off and storm out, but I was running out of ideas.

'*Chok Dee Dur*' I rasped[7] and knocked it back in one. He went back to his tablet, so I played my trump card and undressed in front of him, as seductively as possible. I had cued our favourite sexy song on my iPhone and did my best to impersonate Beyonce, Lady Gaga or whoever it was singing, but the gross bastard still wasn't interested.

'Ying, please leave me alone, I'm playing poker!'

I couldn't believe this, I flipped him the finger and started walking out of the room. Except I didn't even make it to the door.

It was as if I was wading through invisible shit, and slowly sank to the ground and passed out as the bitch on my phone kept repeating the word 'Umbrella -ella-ella'

John

As I stepped over Ying's prone body, I felt nothing but elation, and started to mentally plan the next few days.

Boi had provided me with enough tranquiliser to knock down an elephant in heat, and it had certainly done the trick. I hoped that Ying wasn't going to die, not because I gave a shit, but more because

---

6   **Boom Boom** – *Thai/English slang for having sex.*
7   **Chok Dee Dur** – *Isaan for 'Cheers'.*

of the attention that this would arouse.

Boi was already in the Toyota and, as agreed, he had packed my large suitcase plus his own backpack on the rear seats. He was grinning like a teenager because he knew, if things worked out, he would soon be rich beyond his wildest dreams.

***

Somchai

Seeing that young girl's life so cruelly snuffed out in front of me made me feel that it was a bad omen. I knew that many more would perish on the roads today, but right in front of my house?

Her body was taken away and the louts on the pickup truck had long since fled. The phone that caused her untimely demise was just fragments of glass and metal that spread across the road and into our front yard.

I spent a little time sweeping this bad luck away and thought hard about what I had said to Patty earlier.

She had taken my heart with a single glance all those years ago and now I was selling her off to a man who had long since lost any dignity.

Was I just as bad as he was?

Probably worse.

When I first met Patty, the first thing that she told me was she was carrying another man's child.

A soldier who had given his life for our country.

A hero.

By comparison, what had I become?

Some useless crippled alcoholic with a terrible gambling addiction.

To be honest, Patty was better off without me, but I didn't even have the money or the stones to go anywhere or do anything.

I realised that she had left the house before I had crawled out of my stupor.

I needed to stop this before it ended our marriage, our family, my life.

How could I be so stupid, so greedy, so typical of me?

Our second motorbike was in pieces thanks to a recent pothole incident, so I started walking to the place that I knew Bot and my wife would be. The *short time hotel*[8] was at least a 30-minute jog, so I got a wriggle on and limped as fast as my lame legs would carry me.

Bot

I got the shock of my life when Patty sent me the text. Just like her, it was direct and to the point.

It read '50,000 baht, meet me at Chang Li hotel in one hour.'

She meant business, and this was potentially the best New Year's Day treat I would ever receive.

I made some bullshit excuse to my wife Mali, and after having an extensive shower and shave, I headed off to Chang Li.

Parking outside the drab building, I signalled the reception with my lights, and the huge curtain opened just enough for me to drive inside the inner sanctum and exit the vehicle without being seen by prying eyes. They handed me the key and my heart started to beat a little faster.

She was already in the room and opened the door with a resigned look on her face. I started to feel a little awkward as she took my hand and led me to the bed.

Patty was still a gorgeous woman, and even though she was wearing a towel, I could hardly take my eyes of her stunning figure.

As the towel slipped away I was captivated by her breasts and slim legs that seemed to have defied age.

I was hard without even thinking about it, and I struggled to contain my excitement as I was certain I would come before even

---

8   **Short time hotels** – *also known as Curtain hotels, these exists for those who are having extra-marital affairs and the curtains allow the couple to enter the hotel room without being seen leaving their respective vehicles, extremely common all over Thailand.*

touching her velvety thighs.

I approached her and smelt her hair, I was in heaven and if I had perished that moment, well, all of the trucks and cars and wealth from John wouldn't have mattered one bit.

During that moment, breathing in her beautiful scent, I realised what really mattered in life and I cursed Somchai for his luck all of these years.

She looked into my eyes and started to talk.

I listened and agreed - after all, this was the woman I had lusted for since I could remember having hair on my balls.

Patty

I had planned to leave Somchai for some time in the future, but this indecent proposal, on New Year's Day, had just accelerated that decision. I guess this was as good as time as any, but I still worried about my girls. The money would help, and I knew Ice would be capable of fending for herself, she was the spitting image of Jet and I never doubted her resolve.

I looked this pathetic man on the bed who was offering me a way out of this crappy life. He planned for me to leave Somchai and would install me in the new house as his second wife.

I explained to him that I wanted the money now, and then the sex could commence.

Thankfully, it only lasted less than a minute. I was already showered and on my way out of the rancid little room, as I heard him crying his heart out with some misguided guilty gesture in the form of the well-worn phrase 'I love you'.

To me, this act was the final part of my marriage to Somchai and at least it had empowered me, if only financially, to get away from him forever.

Somchai had never really treated Ice like his own two girls, and this was typical of men, especially entitled Thai men who believed they were worth more than any three women.

I had called my elder sister to come over in the afternoon, and she had been instructed accordingly.

Peng was a hard woman who hated men, she was the perfect adjudicator for my family.

She had been asked to look over the girls, not so much Ice, but ensure that Somchai either pulled his wait or got the hell away from our home.

I spared her the details as I knew her temper was to hot to process the cardinal sin he had committed.

Men, they really are all the same... except for one, who is now long gone.

I wiped away a tear of my own before starting up the motorbike and making one last trip back towards the village.

Ice was serving in the 7-11 and I beckoned for her to come outside for a moment.

I hugged her for what seemed like minutes and then looked her direct in the eye and told her:

'My *Teerak*,[9] do you remember when I told you the tale of *Mae Nak*?'

She could sense something was wrong and nodded silently.

'I need to go and see your grandmother right now and I will not ever be coming back.'

She was shaking by now, so I held her closer.

'Take this money, 40,000 baht, and give it to your Aunt Peng when she comes later today. Your father will be very sad and angry, and you need to be there for him.

You are the strongest person I know, Ice! I need you to do the right thing. Look after your sisters and father, I will pray for you every day, but I can't be here anymore.'

I handed over the envelope, I had removed 10 thousand baht for myself, gave her one more kiss and rode the bike to Buriram City Bus Station.

I texted Somchai to let him know where the remaining family

---

9   ***Teerak** – Thai for Darling.*

vehicle was and walked the short distance to the ticket booth.

'Can I buy a ticket to *On Nut* please?'

The operator didn't look up, burped, then swatted a fly and replied:

'One way or return?'

For the first time in years I felt alive and I replied with some vigour:

'One way – 100%'

He handed over the ticket as if it was no more than a menial task but for me, it was the start of an adventure I should have made nearly 18 years earlier.

I was going to see Jet's family and try and connect with him one final time.

End of Chapter Three

PART II – THE AWAKENING

CHAPTER FOUR — TIME TO LEAVE

Ban Mee, Buriram Province

Ice – Dream Sequence

'Ice! come quick, they are starting to fall!'

Oot's excited voice was loud enough to be heard from half a mile and I sprinted in the direction it was coming from.

I skipped over the rough ground and dodged the tree stumps that had risen above the surface level. Before I reached her, I heard the unmistakeable sound of the large beetles hitting the ground.

She had lit candles under the branches of the Tamarind tree and these tasty insects were literally dropping like flies.

We knew these creatures as Mang Ke Noon and, when fried in oil and a few chillis, they made for delicious eating.

Indeed, the release of flavour as they crackle on your lips is something that mere words cannot describe. It was typical of the poorer families of this region to resort to this particular free cuisine, but they really did taste so amazing. I had heard that the rich people of Isaan and even Bangkok would pay decent money for what used to be their free childhood snacks.

We scurried back to the house and announced our scrumptious bounty to the rest of our family.

But only Nam responded, and I looked towards the road and could see Mum and Dad walking away in the distance.

Instructing my younger sisters to start preparing the beetles, I called out after my parents in vain.

Mum climbed into a large bus that had appeared from nowhere and was waving me goodbye as Dad walked away in the opposite direction.

I sprinted after him but when he turned around, his face was different.

He looked around 20 years old and the features were handsome and strangely familiar.

In fact, he looked like a male version of me.

He was wearing the uniform from an army that had served Thailand many years earlier.

I was about to ask who he was when a pair of shrill voices echoed through my mind.

'Ice, come this way!'

I turned my head to see two female figures about 100 metres away but couldn't make out who they were.

I looked back at the young man, but he had vanished into thin air.

At this point I knew I must be dreaming but carried on relentlessly to the waiting women.

After all, I didn't really want to wake up yet, not after what happened yesterday.

They were walking towards me and then I started to make out their features.

It was Ying and my old friend Nok.

They were both wearing hardly any clothes and appeared to be drunk.

'Ice, it is your time to come and start your new life!'

Both were in good spirits and were puffing away on cigarettes.

They reach out to embrace me but as I held out my arms, they disintegrated in front of my eyes.

'Ice, wake up!'

Oot was standing over me and I cursed the fact that I remained in this house, I was doomed to stay and try to repair this broken family.

She returned to the room she shared with Nam and I climbed out of bed.

After taking a shower, I walked downstairs to see the stern face of Aunt Peng looking daggers right back at me.

'Well, Ice, I guess it's down to me to look after your worthless father and sisters once more.'

Her cruel words were not far off the mark, but I hated the way that she would always seem to think the blame lay with me.

Aunt Peng had once implored her to abort me while there was still time, but how was that my fault?

'Give me the envelope.'

She held out a chubby hand as I retreated to my room under the pretence of looking for the heavy item which was secreted in my jeans pocket.

Sitting down on my bed, I realised now was the time to finally put my plan into action, but first I needed to replay and review what had happened yesterday.

The previous day

Ice

It was early afternoon and the novelty of Songkran had worn off, as it always did. Tonight, I had been invited by Ying to the big party her *farang* was throwing.

I was thinking about whether or not I should go when I noticed that Mum was directly outside the shop.

Her face looked awful and I could see that she had been crying, this wasn't like her. I asked Poon to let me take a few minutes break and rushed out to speak to her.

'Mum, what is it, why are you so upset?'

She hugged me and was sobbing so hard that I had difficulty understanding her.

I pulled away and my top was soaked by her tears, the scene must have been pretty tragic because even the passing kids didn't attempt to throw their water over the pair of us.

'My darling Ice, I have to go, I am so sorry…'

What the hell was she saying to me?

She handed over a heavy thick envelope and continued:

'This is for our family… my sister Peng is coming tomorrow.'

I asked why, and she explained that dad wasn't able to cope, so Peng would stay until he managed.

'But Mum, where are you going?'

She avoided my question and then pulled me closer to whisper into my ear:

'Ice, I have to tell you this, Somchai is not your real father.'

A wave of confusion and pain swept over me, and I could only reply back:

'Mum, what are you saying to me?'

Now I was crying in unison.

'Your father's name was Jet, and he was killed in the army about seven months before you were born. Somchai is a good man, but I believe he never really accepted you as one of his own…'

Now things make a little more sense.

'I'm going down to Bangkok to see Jet's mother, and I don't know if I am ever coming back.'

She told me that Jet was killed in combat before they could marry, and ever since she heard this terrible news, she had never fully recovered. She needed closure, and the only way she knew how was to see if Jet's mother was still alive.

'I will contact you when I arrive and leave a number, but please be strong for Somchai and your sisters.'

I tried to reply but that was it, in an instant Mum had gone.

She didn't tell me about the other ugly incident, which I only learned of a year later.

I had no idea where the money had come from.

'Ice come back inside; I need a break too!'

I returned to my job, and for the rest of the day I worked like a robot. It was such mundane work that I managed to fumble through until 6 pm.

I walked home and didn't bother going to the party, because according to my sisters, it was a bit of a farce.

They had sneaked out whilst Dad… I mean, Somchai, was sleeping off his hangover. They told me that he'd disappeared for most of the afternoon and came back in a right state.

Apparently, by the time they arrive at Ying's house, most of the guests had left because she was going bat shit crazy. As well as insulting pretty much everyone there, she'd thrown most of the food onto the floor and was smashing windows like a crazed bitch.

Not bothering to find out what her problem was, they'd salvaged a few plates of food and snuck back home.

Present day

Ice

I was just about done with the previous day's events when I heard Peng shouting for me to bring down the money.

Then my phone started buzzing and I read the text message. It was from my old friend Nok and although only two words, the contents would change my life forever:

'Come now!'

I removed two thousand baht from the envelope, laid one note under each pillow of my sleeping sisters, kissed them both on the cheek, grabbed my last two days takings from 7-11 and went downstairs.

'Give me money!'

Such a rude bitch! Peng's hand was outstretched for the envelope, and I knew she would pilfer more than her fair share before spending a penny of it on the remaining trio of my family.

So, I tossed it onto the floor out of her reach, forcing her to get her huge arse off the chair, flipped her the finger and walked out of my home with nothing but the clothes on my back and a few baht in my pocket.

I sensed she was screaming obscenities after me, but I just cranked up the volume on my phone and listened to Sek Loso at full volume as I walked towards the nearest transport that would take me to Buriram City.

***

Ying

My eyes seemed to open mid dream, and I wondered if the last evening had been nothing but a hideous nightmare. As I looked around me and saw the smashed glasses, plates and food strewn across the perfect lawn, those hopes were soon dashed to infinity and back.

My head was pounding and I tried my best to recall the events that led to this humiliating event. I must have blacked out as I was sprawled under one of the tables and my skin was burning from the scorching sun.

Checking my phone, I recoiled as I saw it was now early afternoon.

Holy shit, how long had I been out for?

I could hear voices and for a moment I wondered if John and Boi had decided to come back, but it was just a few local boys who were peering over the hedge to get a look of my exposed pants.

I was near-naked, so I grabbed the nearest tablecloth and scrambled across the debris to the front door. After a long bath, I reflected on exactly what had happened on New Year's Day.

The previous day

I recall blacking out after drinking that whiskey John had prepared for me, it must have been spiked with some tranquiliser of sorts.

When I regained consciousness, it was mid-afternoon and I felt groggy as hell. The house was silent, and I had a terrible feeling in my guts that I was alone.

After calling his number, I tried Boi's, but neither fucker picked up.

I got on my bike and did a quick round of the village; the only good news was that I learnt Yam had been killed earlier that day.

I felt no pity for that bitch because if she hadn't been sniffing around my man, she would still be alive. I started to laugh out loud at the bittersweet irony that karma had dished out to that corpse, until I started to think more about my situation.

Where were they?

I returned to the house and after a short nap, I woke up with a start as I remembered the party John and I were going to be throwing today.

There was a loud knock on the door and I sprinted over, expecting John or Boi, or maybe both of the little shits.

Instead, it was the catering company, so I instructed them to get to work and went to the bedroom to start getting myself ready.

By 5 pm, guests were arriving, and I was shocked to see that John seemed to have invited half of the Buriram social elite. He was obviously trying to impress these influential people, but where was the fat bastard himself?

An hour later, neither Boi nor John had appeared. This was starting to really piss me off, I was knocking back the booze and the boring conversation of these high society guests was almost too much to bear. I yearned for the *sanuk*[1] of my friends back in Pattaya and

---

1   **Sanuk** - *Although it is believed that sanuk is the Thai word for fun, it goes way deeper than that. Thailand is the only country in the world where you can experience this unique feeling. You will often see people so poor that they don't really know where their next meal is coming from yet they still retain the ability to laugh and smile. It's a mentality that has the ability to carry you through the most hideous or dangerous experience and help you through to the other side.*

found it very hard to keep my language polite.

The whole event was way too *riab roi*[2] for a common country girl and I started to think of reasons to wrap the party up early.

That was when the whole thing went absolutely nuts.

I could hear my mobile phone ringing and went inside to answer it.

Boi's name was on the screen so excitedly accepted the call.

'Where the fuck are you?'

There was no reply so I continued my tirade:

'The party started hours ago, are you with John?'

Still nothing, so I decided to break the news about his bitch.

'The only good thing that's happened today is that your girl got killed in an accident. She doesn't look so hot now...'

Finally, some response:

'Listen Ying, me and John are in Cambodia, and we aren't coming back.'

That was the end of the call.

I threw the brand new iPhone out of the door and heard some commotion.

It had hit the chief of police square on the nose and there was blood everywhere.

All eyes were on me but instead of apologising, I went totally berserk.

'Everyone please fuck off!'

I started smashing plates, throwing food and generally behaving like a lunatic. Dad tried to restrain me but got a bowl of hot soup thrown in his face for his trouble.

---

2   **Riab Roi** - *Literal translation for this often-used term is a mixture of 'tidy' and 'correct'. When a person or a situation is described as Riab Roi, it speaks volumes about the trouble that they have gone to ensure that everything has been done to ensure all of the etiquette and tradition boxes are well and truly ticked. It's not exclusive to the rich or high-society people of Thailand, even the lower classes place a high value on this calculated action.*

The guests didn't hang around, and after a few minutes I was alone with my tantrum, laughing like an idiot.

Present Day

I shuddered as each and every detail came flying back from my subconscious memory.

There was no coming back from the shame I had caused, so John's chances of hanging with the movers and shakers of Buriram were finished.

But… hang on.

He wasn't coming back, so why the hell should I care?

I paced around the house desperately trying to think of my next move and then it came to me.

To hell with this shithole of a *chonabot*[3] village, I was going to revert to type.

I was a whore and a bloody good one.

I laughed again, but this time it was a positive one, and I grabbed some paper and a pen and started to plan my exit from Isaan once and for all.

I was going home, not here, but my real one, where my type really belonged.

***

Somchai

When I saw that poor girl crushed yesterday morning, I just knew that the day was going to awful.

But it was way worse…

Patty was gone, Ice was missing and now this fat cow Peng was

---

3   **Chonabot** - *Translated roughly as country bumpkin, it's a slightly insulting term aimed at the people who live in villages in the North-East of Thailand. Surprisingly even those who used to be Chonabot themselves pour scorn on those who still live in Isaan, how soon they forget…*

living in my house.

She already instructed me that I needed to get a job or I would soon be kicked out. She knew some heavies that would kick the living crap out of me if I put up a fight.

Of course, this was all of my fault, and I ruined the moment when I came up with that stupid plan to let my wife sleep with Bot.

I did my best to stop that happening, but by the time I limped to the hotel, the deed had been done. Patty was long gone and Bot was also not there.

When I got the text from her to say the motorbike was parked up by Buriram Bus Station, I knew that I had lost her.

I was already sick of the nagging bitch Peng, so decided to get some air.

It was then that I noticed Bot driving past my house but it wasn't the new Toyota he was in; it was that crappy old Nissan that must have been 30 years old.

He saw me and kept his head down as the old vehicle creaked down the road. I found this highly interesting, so I decided to go to the pub and ask the locals what had happened.

It almost cheered me up when I heard the news.

His slut daughter had been totally duped by her *farang* husband.

It was usually the other way around…

He'd left her, and taken her boyfriend as well, just to rub salt in the wounds.

But instead of moping around, the sly bitch had sold her house and Bot's pickup truck for a bargain price and scuttled back to Pattaya.

I chuckled and almost smiled until I remembered that I was in an even worse situation.

I was later to learn that the young girl crushed on her bike yesterday was the other girlfriend of Boi, who was the real boyfriend of Ying, what the fuck was it with people these days?

I almost felt pity for John when I realised my own predicament.

Now where was that cold beer I opened earlier?

***

On the road, near Buriram City

Ice

The bus to Buriram was as uncomfortable as I could remember and I was surprised to see that Songkran celebrations had all but disappeared. Then I remembered the Government announcing that this year, instead of several days, we could only throw water for 24 hours due to severe water shortages.

I struggled to understand how a country with an entire monsoon season couldn't manage to harness at least some of this natural resource for situations exactly like this?

I loved my country but as I grew older I could see a lot of issues that placed Thailand as a developing nation, and the blame would lay directly at those in higher places than I could ever aspire to reach.

Here I was, most probably going to be working in a bar for the foreseeable future, yet I was pontificating about how our government had screwed up - how jumped up was I?

I prayed for Mum and my sisters on that journey. As for Somchai, right now I couldn't give a shit whether he lived or died.

I also thought about Jet, my real father and how different my life could have been if his life wasn't so cruelly snatched away in combat.

Despite being less than 30 kilometres away, I had only visited Buriram a few times, and the bus was certainly in no hurry, stopping almost every few minutes.

By the time we hit the city limits, it was standing room only as we were packed in like sardines. Chickens were everywhere, and I even saw a huge basket of crabs at the front; poor things were bound by rubber bands and must have been slowly suffocating.

Every window on the bus was open, and I could sense we were not far from the station, as the sights and smells swiftly changed from

93

open plains and fresh air to smoky fumes and congested roads.

I felt a little nervous as I really didn't have a clue what lay ahead, I just knew that this was my path now and I was going to follow it the best that I could.

As the bus groaned to a halt, a few chickens were tossed into the air and the patience that Thai people were supposedly famous for was very much absent. I stayed in my seat and waited until the last passenger disembarked before leaving the bus.

I half expected to see Nok waiting anxiously for me, but apart from a few dodgy looking taxi drivers, there was nobody. The day had started to slip into early evening, but the temperature was still as punishing as ever.

Typically for a bus station, there was a small restaurant, so I sat down on a ridiculously flimsy plastic stool and tried to catch the waitresses' attention.

Five minutes later, I was still waiting. 'Screw this' I thought and proceeded to help myself to some water from the oversized fridge.

Eventually, she decided to shuffle over with the dirtiest menu I had ever seen and shoved it under my nose. I ordered stir-fried chicken with basil and boiled rice and grabbed another drink, a beer this time.

I had never drank alcohol, but this seemed as good a time as any because, after all, it was a new start and I was not a child any more.

The food came surprisingly quickly and was delicious, although I wish I could say the same for my beverage of choice. I chose Beer Chang as it was what everyone else seemed to enjoy. It felt unpalatable at first, but to be fair, after the second or third slug, it was not too bad.

I checked my watch and it was just after five in the afternoon, Nok was supposed to meet me here at four…

I decided on more beer and pretty soon, after the third, I was pretty shit-faced. I was less than 50 kilograms, so my tolerance was almost non-existent.

'Hey *nong sao*. Can we sit here with you?'

I smelt his breath before I heard his words. Looking up, I had to try my best to not show fear, as I realised I was surrounded by no less than five rough looking men.

I guessed they were about Somchai's age, but this motley bunch were a different breed altogether. Dressed in leather with tattoos and earrings, nose piercings and practically every other visible place seemingly pierced - these were bad men, no doubt about that.

I didn't have time to respond as they joined my table and started raising merry hell.

I felt a hand on my breast and another started pulling on my jeans.

'Please, I beg you, leave me alone!'

I screamed, shocked at the volume of my own voice, but it had zero effect on these bastards.

Two of them were sharing a Yaba pipe. I looked desperately to the waitress and cook for some assistance, but they refused to meet my pleading eyes.

The table was thrown up in the air and I was being pinned to the filthy floor. I said a silent prayer and wondered why the fuck I had ever left my safe village?

The main protagonist had removed my top and my breasts were on display. I managed to hit him directly in the face with my beer bottle, but this only made him more pissed off.

He was forcing his foul tongue into my mouth, and I felt a groping hand being shoved down my pants.

'Just let it happen you fucking *Garee*,[4] you know you love it!'

I wriggled in discomfort as I could feel the hand in my pants start to paw roughly at my vagina.

'Hey, this one is tight, she may even be a virgin!'

I used all of my abdominal strength to stop this beast from getting any further into my womanhood, but I was fighting a losing battle.

So, this was it.

My short-lived career as a dancer at Tawen Daeng was over before

---

4   ***Garee*** – *Rough slang to describe a woman who sells her body.*

it had begun.

If only Nok had been here at the agreed time, well, we would probably be sharing a bowl of noodles in her room.

I resigned myself to my fate and stopped trying to resist.

Then I shook as I could hear a gun being fired into my attackers.

The huge man holding my chest seemed to arch his back and he fell to the side of me.

The other four sprang up, with fear and loathing in their bloodshot eyes.

'Get the fuck away from her if you want to live!'

I heard a familiar voice and scrambled to my feet, quickly covering up my naked chest with a stray tablecloth.

The men had gone, two of them dragging the bleeding would-be rapist off, ignoring his squeals of pain as blood poured out of a large wound in his leg.

I looked at the person holding the gun and felt a massive wave of relief shake through my aching body.

It was Ying!

***

On the road, somewhere in Nong Kai Province

Somluk

After we left Bank's village, I wasted no time in gunning back towards Nong Kai and allowed him the luxury of a few hours' sleep. I was starting to think that I would have been better off solo, because the memories of Kwan were fresh in my mind.

Wannee had called at least a dozen times and eventually I turned the damn phone off. We hit the blue-eyed girl's village before dark and as Bank awoke, I looked for a hotel near the spot where we had almost killed the stupid cow.

'Where are we?'

Shit, even his voice resembled the pitiful whine of Kwan and I ignored him as I parked up. We got a cheap couple of rooms, and I slowly started to get a good feeling about this project. After some food, Bank and I did a circuit of the village, which admittedly was big enough to be a town, and started asking some questions.

Bank

Somluk had changed a lot since the days we used to hang out together. He'd transformed from an easy-going guy into a real uptight bastard. I understood the importance of this mission and realised that I had replaced a dead man. We'd both be screwed if we came back empty handed, and I had heard many bad things about Wannee's reputation. There weren't many female *Mangdas*,[5] but she was as bad as they came. We must have stopped by at least six or seven hangouts showing the photo of the girl, and each time we were met with a blank stare.

We decided to have a few beers, my idea, and this proved to be rather a good idea. It was an outside coffee shop that served alcohol and food, and both were good quality.

I was staring across the road, and as my eyes wandered around mindlessly, I saw her.

She was even more beautiful than Somluk had said, and her photo certainly didn't hold a candle to this gorgeous vision less than ten metres away from us.

'Somluk!'

I shouted at the top of my lungs, loud enough for everyone, including the target to hear.

'She's there!'

He looked up and we started to run over to the girl.

She was no idiot and also started running as fast as she could.

The race was on, all three of us literally running for our lives.

***

---

5   *Mangda* – *literally, water beetle; however, in this context, slang for pimp.*

Buriram City

Ying

I moved quickly after realising that John and Boi had made a fucking mug out of me. I knew a few people up in Buriram with money and didn't waste time in accepting a shit load of baht for the car and house.

Although the combined value was around 10 million, I accepted around half of that because I needed to get gone that day. I didn't waste time saying goodbye to my family, and they could like it or lump it, because it was me who earned that money, not them.

After all, mum never accepted the fact that I was now the family's main breadwinner and dad, well, he was just a greedy little shitbag.

Everything was signed over, so I got a taxi to Buriram with plans to revisit a few haunts before flying down to Bangkok and then on to my real home.

Pattaya... the only place where I felt like I belonged. Among the bars, the punters and the girls who were just like me.

I booked my flight for the following afternoon, deposited my huge chunk of cash in the Bangkok Bank and left enough for a few weeks of hellraising.

Once I had checked into the best hotel, nothing special compared to Bangkok or Pattaya, I called a few friends and made arrangements for later.

But the most important call I made was to a thug named Pornchai - he was the type of man who could get you anything you wanted or needed.

My wants and needs were specific.

I needed a gun.

Vowing to never again be made of fool of or be beaten by a man, I understood that the only way to achieve this was to have the upper hand.

He provided me with a handgun, a fake Magnum apparently, along with 100 bullets.

It was already loaded, and as he handed it over, I started to feel a warm excitement that could only be compared to a heady mixture of sex and drugs, but more powerful than either.

This heavy tool in my hands was capable of wiping out lives, ruining families and more.

But for me, it was what I needed to feel safe and alive again.

I placed the piece in my real Louis Vuitton handbag and left the hotel with a buzz running through my veins.

I had no intentions of firing this deadly weapon, but less than ten minutes later, that was exactly what I had done.

I had seen the gangsters attacking that young girl by the bus station and, instinctively, was about to cross over the road when I recognised her voice pleading for mercy.

It was Ice!

I was in two minds about engaging with this situation, because even though I was fond of her, these were dangerous men, and I was just one woman.

But I was now one woman with a fucking great, big, loaded gun.

I pulled out the pistol and simply pulled the trigger as I levelled it in the direction of the soon-to-be rape scene.

I shouted a few threats and to my surprise, the largest of the men, the one directly on top of Ice, fell over backwards and the rest of the scumbags dragged him away.

'E-Dok,[6] we will find you and kill you!'

Empty threats perhaps, but I wasn't going to hang around and find out.

This was the detritus of Thai society hung out, and I wondered what the hell Ice, a simple village girl, was doing on their turf?

I grabbed her arm and we ran in the opposite direction to the gang. Luckily, they were out of sight soon enough, and I helped her into the hotel side door and up to my room.

Understandably, she was shaking with fright, and as I fixed us both

6   **E-Dok** – *Isaan slang for 'Golden Flower', yet another term for prostitute.*

a stiff drink I could smell the beer on her breath.

'Ice, what the fuck are you doing here, you stupid little girl?'

Ice

I was still I shocked when Ying started shouting in my face.

Okay, it was a stupid thing for me to do, to get myself into that dangerous situation, but it's not every day that you find out that the person you loved as a father was nothing of the sort. Add to the mix the fact that Mum had probably walked out of my life, it was a real shitty year already.

Despite having handled everything more maturely that I'd have anticipated so far, I knew I needed all the friends I could get, so I turned on the waterworks and tried my best to get some sympathy from Ying. In my opinion, it was a great performance – after all, I'd been through a whole damn lot in such a short timeframe.

When it was over, I was sobbing into the hotel pillow and waited for the hugs to come, but instead there was a slow handclap and a sneer coming from her pretty face.

'Oh, you poor little baby, does nobody love you anymore?'

I could hear the sarcasm in her voice, how she could be so tough to crack?

She then grabbed me and really started to shake me hard, throwing me onto the floor, and opened the bottle of whiskey before taking a huge slug directly from the source.

I then spent a good ten minutes listening to how her day had been even worse and about how we girls should say 'fuck off' to men in future and to our families.

I learnt that she had also been tossed away like a piece of trash by husband and boyfriend, and now she was going to show me how it really was.

My phone interrupted this sermon and I saw Nok's name flash on my screen.

Ying grabbed the device out of my hand and threw it across the room.

She really was angry with me, with herself and with the world in general.

I figured Nok could wait and climbed back on the bed, accepted the glass of whiskey she poured and listened intently.

***

Ban Dek, Nong Kai Province

Somchai

She was bloody fast, but I remembered that Bank was the best runner in our school, and he eventually did justice to that memory by taking her out with a rugby tackle that sent the pair of them sprawling across the pavement.

'Get off me, you fucking *bok hee-ah!*'[7]

I chuckled as I remembered she was a feisty one, the blue-eyed bitch.

There was a bit of a crowd but nobody had the balls to stop it as we dragged her back to the van.

We drove back to the hotel, where Bank ran inside and got our bags as quickly as possible.

We had to get the fuck out before any police arrived.

He held her in the back of the car, and I drove for about 20 minutes before finding a dirt road to turn onto.

Only when I was sure that we were out of range of the main road, I slowed down to a stop.

'Everything okay back there, *puen*?'[8]

Bank replied with some trepidation:

'Err, are you sure this is the same *ying*[9] that you saw before?'

---

7   **Bok hee-ah** – *Insult meaning the male version of 'Common water monitor lizard'.*

8   **Puen** – *Friend.*

9   **Ying** - *Slang for woman/girl, shortened version of Poo-ying, which has the same meaning.*

What the fuck was he saying?

'Of course, what is the problem, isn't she a beauty?'

There was a pause and then he blurted out:

'Yeah she is *suay mahk mahk*,[10] but there is one problem…'

I couldn't believe my ears.

'So, tell me for God's sake, what is wrong with her?

'Nothing except for one fact… her eyes are as brown as your mother's shit!'

Bank

While it was true that I was a novice compared to Somchai and that this was my first job as an unofficial member of the CFC, I am not colour-blind. This girl had such a high price tag on her head because of the supposed colour of her eyes.

I used Somchai's phone torch app to have a good look and took a few photos while I was at it. These were typical brown eyes and, although I had to admit, she was a lovely girl, she didn't have the eye colour that Somchai had been hoping for.

He climbed over the seat, absolutely furious at the poor wench and started ranting about how this was the end of the road for her, me, and him.

Apparently, she was wearing blue contact lenses when they first saw her.

Still holding his Nokia, I tried saving the photos and sent a few to my own phone using the contacts list, which was deep inside my overnight bag. Strangely enough, I didn't hear any acknowledgement beep, but wasn't really that concerned, as I could see that the girl herself was starting to go into one.

Somchai reached over and punched her in the face at least three times and that put an end to her little strop.

'We have to kill her and then get the hell out of here!'

---

10   **Suay mahk mahk** - *Literal translation means 'very beautiful'.*

She went limp and blood was bubbling out her nostrils.

I thought death was a little harsh, especially as she was so lovely, but he was the boss.

We had made quite the scene back there, and who knows what would happen next, especially as she looked quite wealthy judging by her clothes, jewellery and demeanour. Sure, she could swear with the best of them, but kids today, they just didn't seem to care about respect…

With speed and agility, Somchai removed her gold and slit her young throat with his blade before I could even suggest that we have some fun with her first.

He produced a shovel and I was instructed to dig a shallow grave for the unlucky Isaan girl whose name we didn't even know.

Less than an hour later we drove to the Laos border, without a word between us. We were not bad men, just desperate, and another death wouldn't make much of a difference. At least that's what I liked to believe.

Somchai's phone started ringing in my pocket and I asked him what to do.

'Just let it fucking ring, you imbecile!'

That was a bit much I thought, but I turned the call off only to find a text already sitting in the inbox.

Curiously, I opened it and saw the name 'Rambo' as I read the contents.

What I read next filled me with dread.

'Somchai, who is Rambo?'

He stood on the brakes and looked me straight in the eye. I could see the fear in his eyes and knew then that we were both dead men.

'He's Wannee's hitman, why?'

Realising that I'd sent the photo of the now dead girl to Rambo instead of myself, his phone slipped my hand and dropped to the floor.

'That girl we just buried, it's his fucking younger sister…'

Buriram City

Ying

I called my old friends to cancel the evening as I felt Ice would end up dead in a ditch if I didn't at least tell her how it is and explain what her options should be.

I was probably wasting time on this girl, but I felt she was worth the effort and maybe it was time I did something good. I wasn't religious, not after the shit I had seen over the last few years but, well, I believed in karma. Maybe this was my way of ensuring my own luck changed?

I smiled as she recoiled from her first shot of Johnny Walker Black Label nearly retching and I guessed that she had never been near this drink before. She was very cute, even though her clothes were pretty crap and she had zero make up on.

'First of all, Ice, are you one-hundred-percent sure that you are ready for this?'

She nodded and I knew that, like me before, she couldn't go home, not until she had scratched this itch good and proper.

I went at lengths to explain that although tough, Buriram is nothing compared to Bangkok or Pattaya. She needed to become harder and remember two things that all people in *The Industry* religiously believed and lived by:

1. Money is number one!
2. Family is next!
3. Look after your body because this is how you get to number one!
4. Trust no men, Farang or Thai!

At least that was what I believed, and even though I was licking my wounds, it was exactly that mantra that kept me alive.

'We are Thai women, and that means we are always below men in the pecking order, the fact that we are poor makes it even harder. But we have something, something between our legs, that gives us the ability to earn a lot of money! Thai men know this and they will find you and leech off you as long as they can!'

I was quite enjoying this one-way lecture and wondered, if only for a split second, if I could have made it as a teacher, well if I hadn't left school myself at fifteen?

Ice was listening, but I doubted that she was really taking it in.

We spent quite a few hours talking about our families, the hard lives we had both endured, and I was starting to grow very fond of her as I could see that we had so much in common right up until the day I left home.

She had tears in her eyes when I explained that my father had molested me as a young teenager and how mum had tried to stop him, only for him to laugh and carry on.

Her stepfather seemed to be less of a pervert but, as he wasn't her real father, surely that time would come.

I escaped having sex with my own Dad, but then I started to understand that many of my friends were going through the same thing. So, one night, he came for me after a drinking session, and I was prepared.

As he climbed into my bed, I produced a razor, held the sharp blade to his balls, and explained in no uncertain terms that next time they would be removed and fed to the pigs we reared in the back yard.

That seemed to do the trick, but I never allowed myself to be alone with him again.

I hated Thai men, and foreign men were just as bad, but at least they paid to have sex with me.

I realised too late that John was only playing me and I swore to myself that this time in Pattaya, I would call the shots. These were more than empty words, because now I had serious cash in the bank and I had plans, I just wasn't sure of what they were yet.

Ice listened and when I asked her to come with me, I could see she really wanted to, but something was holding her back. She had decided to stay here in Buriram for now, and maybe she'd eventually make that giant leap into the real bar scene.

We shared the bed and in the morning I got up early, showered, dressed and left twenty thousand baht on the table with a note for Ice.

In less than three hours I was back in my real home.

I was back in Pattaya, where I belonged.

End of Chapter Four

CHAPTER FIVE – WELCOME TO THE RED SUN[1]

---

1   **Red Sun** – *Tawen Daeng is often regarded as such.*

Buriram City

Ice

I awoke with a thumping headache and for a few moments, I wished deeply that I were back home in my own bed.

For a few seconds I imagined the familiar and safe scents of my sheets and teddy bears that had been my sentinels and companions since I was young enough to believe they were my friends.

But this was a hotel room and I was struggling to piece together the parts of the previous day that had led to me being here, alone.

I then started to recall the attack at the bus station and how my brave Ying had fired a bullet into the main protagonist and how that action had surely saved my life.

By the looks of things, my hero had long since left this room and I was shocked to find a letter and twenty thousand baht in used notes on the bedside table.

Was this to be a feature of my life? People who I was forced to rely on would just up and leave when they were bored?

But she really was my guardian angel and, as I took a shower, I remembered the somewhat one-way conversation that we shared, along with a bottle of whiskey, until the sun was rising in the sky.

Ying had asked me to join her on her return to Pattaya and made a very convincing case, but I was here for Nok, and she understood. She had developed a hatred of men since her last deceitful relationship. I had to stifle an urge to laugh when she thought nothing of the way her and Boi planned to fleece John, her farang husband/benefactor.

I guess I was still far too naive to understand that foreign men weren't our equal.

According to Ying, they were so far down the pecking order that eventually, she just saw them as a means to get money and whatever else was on offer.

Curiously, I asked her if the sex was one of the reasons she loved her job. She almost fell off the bed laughing and went to some lengths to explain that not only do *farang* men stink to high heaven, but most of them don't know how to make love to a woman.

This puzzled me because I used to wonder about how it would be to have sex with Brad Pitt or Johnny Depp, I never realised that they were probably just smelly and useless idiots, as Ying had described them.

I did have a sneaking suspicion that these were most likely bitter words from a woman who had been twice used and scorned within the last 48 hours. Still, she had saved my life and gifted me a considerable amount of money, so who was I to argue?

I checked out of the hotel, surprised to see that it was already midday, hailed a motorbike taxi to the Tawen Daeng and went to meet Nok.

✳✳✳

Pattaya City

Ying

It had been a while since I was single and after the twin betrayal I had just experienced, I needed to get laid, and that was the only thing on my mind.

I checked into the Hard Rock Hotel and ignored the looks and whispers that came as, true to form, they treated all single and attractive Thai woman as if they were no more than whores.

Of course, in my case they were correct, but I doubted that the combined wealth of all six bitches working in reception amounted to what I had in the bank at that exact moment.

The irony of it was that the decent looking ones working behind the desk would probably be working the beach road after their shift to try and get some nefarious earnings of their own.

'Excuse me madam, I think we don't have any rooms for a single night.'

Cheeky little bastard, I guess they thought I needed the room for my customers, how fucking dare they?

I pulled about sixty thousand baht from my purse and looked on as their eyes almost popped out onto the reception counter.

'You are excused *Nong Sao*, now be a good little receptionist and find me a room for the rest of the month…'

That had the desired effect, and pretty soon these salary slaves couldn't do enough for me.

I tipped the porters each with a shiny red 100 baht note and threw myself on the king-sized bed like a picture book princess instead of the horny little bitch I really was.

***

Buriram City

Nok

It had been a good two years since I had laid eyes on Ice, and as she jumped off the back of the motorcycle taxi, I had to catch my breath because she was so gorgeous.

Without so much as a lick of makeup, she had such clear skin and full lips that I almost fancied her myself. Above all, she had that innocence that had long since deserted me and most of the friends who shared the same occupation.

I gave her a mock curtsy and then ran over for a full hug.

'Welcome to the Tawen Daeng *Nong-Sao*, I have missed you so much!'

This was genuine, it had been way too long. I never returned to the village after my parents had moved away, and Ice was the only soul who I stayed connected with.

'What the hell are you wearing, and is that whiskey I can smell?'

She was giggling and started telling me some story about how Ying, an older girl I knew from the industry, shot a would-be rapist when she was waiting for me at the bus stop.

I wasn't sure if this was true but it probably was, I apologised for missing the rendezvous and explained that my boyfriend had been unwell. The truth is that Sombat is a drug addict and I was head over heels in love with him, despite this minor personality flaw.

'Let me show you where you will be staying, you can have my old bed...'

Ice

Nok looked at least five years older than I'd remembered her, but still was as friendly as ever. I could sense some sadness and maybe a little fear when she described her boyfriend, I wondered if there were actually any decent ones left?

She gave me a mini tour of the Tawen Daeng establishment and I was shocked to see how large the main room actually was. As she showed me to my quarters, I felt a pang of disappointment as I had expected us to be sharing living space.

I was introduced to the other three room occupants, and when I noticed they all had the same name as me, I sensed that I wasn't exactly welcome. I almost did a double take when taking a quick look at their Tawen Daeng tags, the four of us were all called Ice!

My own uniform was then flung at me as if I were a stray dog being offered a blanket for the night.

I looked at my own name tag and it bore the name 'Ice 4'.

This wasn't how I had played the scene out in my mind and even Nok was shuffling uncomfortably. She then made some excuse about going to see her man and disappeared leaving me with the terrible trio of Ice wannabees.

'*E-dok*! Just our luck to be stuck with a *Chonabot* who can't even have an original name!'

I ignored the insults and laughed to myself at the irony of these stupid girls. None of them looked like much, so I just put this animosity down to good old-fashioned jealousy.

I was later to learn that this trio of miscreants had their claws in quite a few pies and would be forced to use considerable force in dealing with their vicious ways.

'Ladies! Please come to the main room, it's time for another evening of fun!'

This massive voice echoed through the rooms and I was pushed aside by the three bitches so threw on my uniform, which was a little tight, and followed them into the 'arena'.

Nok

I felt like shit for leaving Ice there, especially with those three ratbags sharing the same breathing space, but what could I do? Sombat had called me and he needed me right now more than Ice did. Anyway, she had to grow up, and I was sure she'd deal with that pathetic gang.

I jumped on my motorbike and instead of heading towards his room, I gunned the vehicle towards the bus station.

I hated this part of town, especially after dark, and as I killed the engine I shivered involuntarily when I spotted the man with a limp shuffling towards me. I handed over the 500 baht note and in return got a tiny package wrapped in silver foil.

Less than five minutes later I opened Sombat's door to see him shaking like a leaf.

'Did you get it?'

He was snarling at me and instead of showing concern I just flung the *Yaba* towards him and slammed the door.

What the hell had he become? This wasn't the handsome and eloquent man who I fell in love with almost one year ago.

Sombat was the guitarist in one of the most popular bands in Tawen Daeng, and it was love at first sight.

Well, it was for me anyway.

I knew he was using *Yaba*, but that didn't put me off at first, until it seemed he was spending his money and mine on getting smashed on this stuff.

Once I tried to deny him the drug. That was when he punched me so hard that I had to take three nights off because of my black eye. The next time he hit me in the stomach, as he realised that we would both suffer if I couldn't earn money.

Eventually, his guitar and amplifier were sold to pay for this vice, at which point I started to understand that this was no longer the same man that I was mesmerised by on the Tawen Daeng stage that night last year.

I rode back to Tawen Daeng to see how Ice was doing, because I could not bear to look at this wreck of a human being any longer.

Ice

For some reason I expected to see at least forty servers lining up to start work, the place was just so massive. I guessed at least one thousand individuals would fit inside this establishment. So, when it appeared that less than a dozen were working here, I started to get a handle on the sheer volume of work that lay ahead.

Before the doors opened, we were ordered to carry out a basic cleaning duty that involved sweeping the floor and polishing the tables.

I did a fair bit of sweeping up the dozens of old cigarette ends that were stuck to the discoloured carpet, but this only added more filth to the already disgusting surface.

After about 30 minutes, the lights suddenly dimmed and the music started to play. I became aware of the customers who started to arrive and followed the rest of the servers at the bar.

Feeling like a rabbit stuck in the headlights of an oncoming car, I was handed a menu and pushed in the general direction of a table that already had four occupants.

As I approached and looked a little closer, I was shocked to see that these were four foreign men, all looking directly at me. My uniform was feeling as if it would split at the seams, but that didn't seem to concern this handsome quartet.

The only time I had ever spoken to a *farang* was in school, and he was at least fifty years older than these guys, one of them even looked a little like Brad Pitt!

Trying in vain to avoid making eye contact, I flung the menu on the table and produced my pen and notepad that had been handed to me a few minutes earlier.

They tried to order in their own language, which I presumed was English, but I had no idea what the hell they were saying. This amused them and eventually they pointed to the Chang beer and 'Brad' held up four fingers with a cheeky grin besides.

I started to wonder what those fingers would feel like all over my naked breasts and scurried off to the bar for my first ever order, with a weird but not unpleasant feeling in my pants.

I shouted the order in and was already a little unsteady on my feet as the four bottles of beer were heavier than I had anticipated. I only got a couple of steps in when I felt a rough shove in my back and I went flying to the ground.

The beers were past saving, and as I looked up, I saw the three ugly Ice sisters sneering down at me as if I was where I belonged, amongst the stale cigarettes and multitude of dried bodily fluids on the floor.

This was about the limit of my patience, and I grabbed the closest bottle with the intention of breaking over the nearest Ice's head, when a hand took my wrist and gently removed the weapon.

It was Brad!

Nok

As I entered the building, I could see that some drama had already unfurled around Ice and wasted no time in sprinting over to see what the hell was going on. I needn't have bothered because she was being helped up by a young and very handsome *farang*.

The Ice gang were skulking around and I suspected that they were behind the whole thing. When they saw me, all three just walked off, so I had to ask the barman what had happened.

I re-ordered the four beers and carried them over to the thirsty *farang*'s table.

'Nok, thank God you are here, those bitches...'

I cut her off mid-sentence.

'Listen *Nong-Sao*, you are going to have to toughen up real quick or otherwise they will have you for breakfast.'

I noticed the attention I was also getting from the table and flashed my killer smile as I started to think of a way to turn this to my advantage.

After a few words with the barman, myself and Ice beckoned them to a larger table in the elevated VIP area. Without asking, I then ordered a bottle of Chivas Regal with six glasses and mixers.

One way or another, this was going to be my lucky night!

***

Walking Street, Pattaya City

Ying

Aware that there were at least two other bodies in my huge bed, I dragged myself out of the pit and baulked at the state of the room we had partied in last night.

Although still numb, I could recall some of the festivities that led to me being in this state.

I had revisited the gogo bar where I used to work and had been involved in a huge argument with my ex-boss. The old bitch seemed to think that I was on the scrounge and looking for a handout or even my old job back.

Stupid old cunt!

I put up with her rant for about ten minutes as the crowd gathered around us.

It was too early for any customers, but most of the sluts I used to work with were still there, just looking older and more haggard than before.

The great thing for me was I that I knew the *Mamasan* was in a lot of trouble and had already checked on her status before making my entrance.

It was at the point where she tried to slap me when I decided to actually defend myself.

She threw a bony hand towards my cheek and instead of allowing her to make contact, I caught her wrist and simply twisted her arm until she was on her knees. Then I kicked her full in the face several times before dragging her outside by her hair.

Well, it was actually a wig, but you get the point.

I had already alerted several heavies to step in if anything random happened, but there were no police around.

The kicking continued for five minutes until I could see that this old joke had no fight left.

I looked across to the scantily clad audience who were watching this spectacle and shouted out:

'Hey whores! I am the new owner of this bar, anybody who still wants to work here, I suggest you get your scrawny tails inside and shut your fucking mouths!'

I had, behind the scenes, already paid the lease for 'Pussy-a-gogo' for the next two years and was merely popping in for some much needed payback.

Feeling fulfilled, I left the old wretch on the pavement and crossed the street to see some old friends.

Most of the girls in the club I had just taken over were well past their sell-by date. The books told no lies, and I had decided on a total refurb, a new name and, most importantly, all new staff.

The following memories of that night kind of faded but, as I kicked the two men out of my hotel room, I chuckled at the memory of the look in my old boss's eyes as I dealt out that much needed karma with my fists and boots.

Today was going to be the start of a brilliant business career for me here in South Pattaya.

I was back!

***

Buriram City

Ice

We moved to a larger table and once Nok had joined us, it seemed like the party was really starting to kick off. I was next to Brad, and Nok was squeezed next a man called Phil. The two men without any girls seemed to be deep in conversation, despite the incredible volume that Tawen Daeng speakers were pumping out.

'*Khun Cheu arai Teelak?*'[1]

Oh my God, Brad could speak Thai, and he was pretty fluent!

I told him my name was Ice and got the shock of my life when he revealed that his real name was actually Brad!

His arm was around me and, for some reason, I didn't mind one bit.

Nok was already kissing her *farang*. I was feeling lightheaded because I wasn't expecting anything like this.

'Pay bill!'

We looked up to see a stern-faced older lady with a flashlight and a tray with a piece of paper written in both Thai and English.

Nok explained to me and the men that they had to pay in advance for our company.

Brad tossed over a new one thousand baht note without breaking a sweat and continued looking into my eyes as if he was trying to hypnotise me.

Nok explained to me that although Tawen Daeng was not a bar where the girls went with customers, it was allowed to sit with them, so long as they paid for the privilege.

'What happens afterwards?'

---

1   *Khun Cheu arai Teelak – Literal translation for 'Hey, what is your name, Darling?'.*

She laughed and started talking about how it was up to us, when her facial expression changed and she told me to meet her in the toilets. I excused myself and walked over to the toilets near the stage, where I waited a few minutes.

Where was she?

Nok eventually arrived and was just ending what appeared to be a fairly animated phone conversation.

'Ice, are you still a virgin?'

This I wasn't expecting, and I replied with a meek nod of my head.

Nok's face lit up and she was off again on her blasted phone call. I knew she was always a sneaky one but had no clue how her morals and standards had changed since leaving the village.

After having a wee, washing my hands and applying some lipstick, I returned to Brad and his friends.

The whiskey was opened, and by the looks of things, everyone was already feeling the effects. I forced a few down my throat but added a heap of soda water to lessen the effect.

After Nok returned, two more servers appeared and the eight of us were having a merry old time. It was made even more enjoyable when I realised the three remaining Ice's were ordered, by Nok, to serve our table. Their name tags weren't unnoticed by Brad and his friends as they renamed the poor girls in order of their looks and age.

Brad did his best to pay me a lot of attention, and although we kissed several times, his hands never went near my chest or below the waist area. He smelt very nice indeed, and I wondered why Ying had painted such a vile picture of *farang* to me before?

'Okay everyone, lets pay the bill and go to the nightclub!'

Nok seemed keen to move the party along and nobody was complaining.

The bill seemed to be more than I had expected, but Brad's friend Phil paid it without even checking the myriad of chits attached.

Before we left, Brad had explained that the four of them had come over to Thailand to practice Muay Thai. In fact, Brad himself was in training for a fight at the national stadium in Bangkok. The reason for their night out was that they had two months of solid training ahead and needed to let off some steam before starting the vigorous schedule.

I didn't share this information as I couldn't see why Nok needed to know.

The nightclub was on the other side of Buriram City. On our way out, Brad pulled me to one side and we got separated from the rest of the people.

'Ice honey, this is my last night before I get back to training, I am so pleased that I met you, but I wonder if you could do something special for me?'

His English was too fast, so he spoke again in Thai, and I got the gist of what he wanted. I had a feeling that I would see this charming man again, but as he led me in the opposite direction I could hear Nok yelling out for me.

I shouted back to let her know we'd be a little while but was amazed when Brad led me to a tattoo parlour!

He wanted my name on his arm and before I had sat down, the artist was already getting to work.

Less than 30 minutes later he had the Thai script for Ice on his arm
– *Nam keng* – น้ำแข็ง.

I was amazed, such a sign of devotion, this strange night was getting even more bizarre!

Then something even more insane happened, I sat right down and had Brad's name tattooed onto my upper chest! It hurt like hell, but I was in a place in my mind that I never wanted to leave.

About an hour later, as mine took a little longer, we joined the rest of the party at the nightclub, but as we approached the table where Nok, Billy and the rest were sitting, I could feel that the atmosphere had changed.

There were also four Thai men at the table and it seemed as if we had walked in halfway through an argument.

We sat down and Brad started asking Phil what was taking place, when one of the Thai men smashed a glass on the table and started cursing the *farang* in very aggressive Thai words.

Nok

As soon as I saw the four *farangs* in the Tawen Daeng, I knew that I had to call Sombat. It was unusual for foreigners to come to the club, and we had to make hay while the sun shined, or at least the Red Sun!

Thing improved even more when I saw that the most handsome one was all over Ice. This would be very easy indeed!

I decided against telling her what was going to happen, as I wasn't sure that Ice was on the same wavelength just yet. She would understand that these idiots would get what they deserved, and besides, what were they even doing here in Buriram? I guessed they were just young travellers in the wrong place and at the wrong time.

When they started flashing their big money back at our club, I called my love to assemble three or four other friends and to meet us at the night club around midnight.

When Ice and Brad disappeared, I was a little annoyed - after all, he seemed to be richer than his three friends - but they eventually appeared a little later.

The plan was one that rarely failed and here was how it usually played out:

- We go to the club and grab a table.
- After half an hour of heavy drinking, we are joined by Sombat and his crew.
- They order more drinks for the table.
- Once the *farangs* are relaxed, Sombat and his pals add a little extra to the drinks and offer these to the *farangs*.
- The drinks are laced with heavy sedatives.
- Once the drugs have the desired effect, we frogmarch the *farangs* to the nearest ATM and fleece them for as much cash as their cards will stand.

- We leave them on the pavement and go to another club to celebrate the stupidity of these young idiots.

It works every time and nobody gets hurt… well, not unless they are not cooperating. Tonight, however, was turning into one of those times when the *farangs* are just not playing fair.

Before Ice and Brad arrived, Sombat decided to speed things up and added his potion to three of the glasses, slid them towards the three *farangs* and raised a toast.

Except he said something in Thai that one of the foreigners seemed to understand. He whispered to his two friends and as a result, the contents of the drinks were poured onto the floor.

Sombat was furious and, just as Ice and her man arrived, he smashed his own glass onto the table and stood up, swearing as if his life depended on it.

The four *farangs* stood together, Ice was behind Brad and shit was about to go down.

I wasn't worried because, in my experience, Thai men are much better fighters and although this was going to be messy, the end result would be the same.

I shouted above the din and called Ice over.

'Listen, these ignorant fucks refused the drinks and now my boyfriend and his friends are going to give them a beating before taking their money!'

Ice looked at me and I could see mixture of resentment and hurt in her deer-like eyes. It didn't matter right now though, as she had to learn how things worked in the real world.

＊＊＊

Ice

I couldn't believe how evil Nok could be! These nice young men from USA had been so friendly to us, and now she planned to beat and rob them. What the hell had happened to my once lovely friend? Is this what happens when we swap the idyllic village life for the not so big city?

I could only imagine how much worse Bangkok or Pattaya would be by comparison.

I tried in vain to grab Brad's arm to warn him, but the eight men were almost at the club exit already.

Nok pulled me back because she must have seen how angry I was, I managed to break free and sprinted as fast as I could to help Brad and try to break up this fight.

But when I reached the exit door and looked outside, all I could see was the four farang standing over Sombat and his friends.

The club security guy just looked on in shock.

Nok was just behind me and we both listened to his playback of what he'd just seen.

'The white boys kicked their fucking heads in!'

A few more Thai men were lingering but it appeared that none of them wanted to know what else these foreign men were capable of.

According to the door guy, the Thai thugs started the fight, one of them produced a chain and they looked like they were going to dish out a beating until one of the foreigners, Brad, avoided a punch from Sombat and unleashed a spinning kick that dropped his opponent to the ground.

Three more punches and the rest of the would-be thieves were sent to the floor, and they showed no signs of getting up.

I rushed over to Brad but he seemed a little distant.

Did he think I was a part of this?

Before I could ask him, a taxi pulled up and the farang piled in, he didn't even give me a look.

What a night of ups and downs!

When Sombat finally came to his senses, he started slapping Nok around the head until the security guy intervened. He also got a slap for his troubles.

The four Thai men shuffled off, and I hobbled back inside the club, holding Nok, as she was bleeding pretty badly.

Then she turned on me.

'You stupid bitch, why didn't you say they were boxers?'

I was lost for words; she was the one who had planned to rob these innocent men and had even used me as bait!

She got up and walked out of the club, leaving me with a massive bill and absolutely no way of paying for this whole mess.

At this moment in time, I had never missed my little room and my family so much in my entire life.

End of Chapter Five

CHAPTER SIX — TIME TO GROW UP

Buriram City

Ice

My second night at Tawen Daeng was far less dramatic, and I tried my best to buckle down and just get on with this life that I had chosen for myself.

Nok never returned to work after that nightmare of an evening, and it would be a year before I heard from her again.

Brad was like a distant memory and I started to wonder if that would ever develop into something more than just a faded pipe dream.

If I was to remain here at TD, I had to move fast.

Before starting work, I decided I needed to get out of that room I was sharing with my three namesakes and, thanks to the handout from Ying, I secured a tiny apartment less than a ten minute walk from my workplace.

It had a bed, rice cooker and... nothing else really, but at least I had some privacy, so by the time I had to start work, my shattered mood was lifted somewhat.

Of course my night's dreams were filled with imaginary illicit romps with Brad.

I was his dominator, ordering him to service me in a myriad of positions, many probably illegal in Isaan and most of Asia, no doubt.

But in reality, I feared I would see my days out here without nothing as exciting as a cigarette stain adorned in the squalid carpet

I knew so little about life outside of the bubble I had created in the village that I called home and I had to start facing facts.

Nobody was looking after me, I had to step up and take responsibility for myself.

Nok was gone.

Spending some time thinking about that, I could see that her leaving wasn't necessarily a bad thing. She hadn't exactly been a good friend this time around and probably had more on her mind than just looking after me.

Brad was gone.

I still had his name tattooed on my body and I hoped that one day he'd return, but I seriously doubted it. If I could somehow reach out to him, it would only be to say sorry and to tell him to look after himself.

But I imagined he somehow thought I was part of last night's set-up and thinking there would be no way to make him trust me again, I tried my best to wipe that lovely young man from my mind.

I got to work after processing all these thoughts in my head. Apart from a few scowls from my former roommates, it was if last night had never happened.

I also made the decision not to contact my family until I was in a position to financially help them. I hoped the money that evil Aunt Peng was holding could at least sustain them for now, especially my two younger sisters, whom I missed so much.

I half expected Somchai to move on, as many Thai men do when the chips are down.

As for Mum, well I didn't have a clue about what she had been through with Bot at the time and struggled to understand her reasoning for abandoning us.

The weeks seemed to fly by, mainly because I would work until the early hours, get some food, and then sleep for most of the day.

I avoided the temptation to make friends because I knew that they would eventually let me down. But one night, about nine months after I had started work at the Tawen Daeng, all of that changed for me.

I was walking to work on a balmy evening and, as I tried to cross the busy road, a large car slowed down directly in front of me. Naturally, I stopped and moved back a little to allow the vehicle to pass. Instead, it remained static, and the driver wound down his window and started talking to me.

His name was Pap and he was the new entertainment manager at Tawen Daeng.

Recognising him, but not the least bit interested in making a new friend, I ignored Pap and sprinted across the road, almost being clipped by a speeding idiot on a motorbike.

Keeping my head down, I continued to work.

About three hours into my shift, I was taking a much-needed break outside the back entrance when I was aware that someone else was also there.

'Hey Ice, I have been watching you for some time.'

Looking up I recognised that it was Pap and, although he was good looking, I looked at the floor, praying that he would just go away.

But he was persistent.

Offering me a cigarette, Pap moved closer, and it was clear that eventually I would have to speak up.

'I don't like *burree*,[1] sorry.'

Pap simply put the cigarette back in the packet and continued talking until, after five minutes, he went back inside.

Apparently, he had noticed me some weeks ago and was offering me a promotion. Instead of a lowly server, he announced that I was to be elevated into the better paying position of hostess.

The money was good, about 200 extra a night and I had less hours. I gave this little thought, but when I returned to work the next night, he was there waiting for me.

'Okay Ice, you start tonight!'

I was trying to just get through this part of my life without getting

---

1   ***Burree*** – *Cigarette.*

attention, but this persistent man seemed to be ruining my plans!

I pleaded with Pap just to let me be, but he was having none of it. In fact, he told me that if I refused this promotion, my time at Tawen Daeng was going to be terminated.

'So, I have no choice then?'

Pap chuckled and replied:

'Ice, you are a strange one indeed. Many girls, many of them would kill for a promotion like this.'

I had no doubt that this was the case.

He then beckoned for me to follow him to his office. This was just another example of how Thai men manipulated us with their power and influence.

Entering the large room, I had all but resigned myself to being raped by Pap. This may come across as being paranoid and dramatic, but it was the way here in Thailand, especially for younger poor women.

'This is your new uniform, and here is some money to get a makeover.'

He then summoned in another hostess, who explained that my hair and makeup was terrible, and I was to follow her to get this rectified.

'It's okay Nong-Sao, Pap is a good boss and I will look after you.'

Her name was Dada and she was to become a good friend during the rest of my time here at Tawen Daeng.

I was surprised that despite my reticence, I really enjoyed the hour or so of pampering, and after the makeover was complete, I looked into the mirror to see a more confident looking woman than the young girl who had left her village not so long ago.

'Ice, you are very beautiful. I think being a hostess is a job that you were born to do!'

Again, Dada was making me feel comfortable, so I opened up a little and asked her about herself and the new job I was about to start that night. She explained that she'd been working at Tawen

Daeng for a long time but had only just returned from the Kalasin branch where her family were from. She knew Pap for a few years and was recently brought over to Buriram to help him organise the team.

She had spotted me a few days ago and advised Pap that he should offer me promotion straight away.

'Dada, will I have to sleep with customers?'

She looked at me with some amusement and replied:

'Listen Ice, that's totally up to you girl!'

My job duties were to entertain the guests in the VIP area, get the attention of the servers, help with ordering food and generally being the 'go-to' person for that table. In return, I could eat and drink as much as I was offered and should expect a decent tip for a lot less work than in my former job as a server.

I began my new job, which turned out to be a lot more fun than I had expected. I spent most of the time at one table, but I really didn't mind. I got a kick out of bossing the Ice gang around, and when the night ended, I had a huge one-thousand-baht tip without having to put up with any groping from the customers.

As I was leaving the club, it was about 2 am, I heard a voice behind me - it was Dada.

'Hey sexy lady, do you want to go and grab some food with me?'

I looked over and she was alone, so I thought why not?

Dada waved down a taxi, and we sped across town going through some back roads I had never seen before. I fully expected to be taken to some flashy after-hours place, but I couldn't have been further off the mark.

Eventually we stopped outside a run-down row of shops, and I was wondering if she had given the driver the wrong address.

Dada chuckled and after slipping the taxi guy a 50-baht note, she grabbed my arm and we stumbled out of the car.

'Ice, this is my Mum's noodle shop, I called her earlier to see if she could open up for a little while.'

This was just what I needed, I had been feeling so homesick and pretty soon we were chowing down on some of the best Isaan food I had eaten since leaving the village.

It was so good, in fact, that I started crying.

'Ice dear, whatever is wrong?'

Dada and her Mum looked highly concerned, and I explained about how her food reminded me of Mum's own noodles. They asked about my family, and by the time I had finished, all three of us were crying.

'You should go and see them soon.'

Dada was being genuine, but I knew that I still had to work harder and save more money before I could hope to help them properly.

We had a lovely deep fried banana dessert and afterwards, as Dada helped her Mum to clean the dishes, I casually flipped through a copy of the daily newspaper. I had totally lost interest in the affairs of the nation and found myself skimming the back pages where sports took pride of place.

The headline caught my eye but not as much as the large photograph did. It read:

'Foreign boxer retains world Muay Thai title with KO against our best fighter!'

My eyes were glued to the handsome features of this champion boxer from the USA.

It was my Brad!

I screamed with delight until I came to my senses.

This lovely man, this champion, had walked away from me that night and quite rightfully so. As far as Brad was concerned, I was part of that failed trap to rob him and his three friends.

I placed the newspaper back on the table and did my best to wipe him out of my mind and my heart.

Dada invited me to sleep over and we spent what was left of the night watching old movies on her mum's black and white TV set, it was the best time I had experienced since moving here to Buriram.

I settled into my job as hostess and started to enjoy this new lease of life, mainly thanks to Dada and her friendship. Despite a few close calls, I never had to sleep with clients, and as my eighteenth birthday was looming, I did wonder about when I would find the right man to give my virginity to.

I never shared my somewhat rare status to my colleagues or even to Dada.

This was my secret and I would hang on to it as long as I could.

I covered up my tattoo of Brad's name but one afternoon I decided that I had enough saved to treat myself to a small second-hand TV set for around two thousand baht.

Prior to this, I would try and watch movies on my old phone, but the screen was just way too small to enjoy the visual content.

I returned with my prize after a bit of negotiating with the shop's owner and plugged it in with excitement.

I was never a materialistic person but this was actually the first thing of any value that I had bought with my own money. Even at home, mum had rented our television at what turned out to be an extortionate price. That was my first insight into Western culture and, more importantly, Mr Pitt!

When the loan sharks had taken it away, I remember swearing, amidst tears, that I would never be dependent on these vultures who seemed to prey on those who had nothing.

I turned the device on and tuned into Channel Seven for the latest news updates. There was the usual rubbish about wars in far off countries, and it looked like the United States of America had elected yet another total dickhead as their president.

This held no interest for me as I failed to see how any of this affected my boring little life here in Buriram. I was just about to try another channel when the sports update started.

There was a lot of excitement because a huge event was taking place at the Lumpini stadium in Bangkok.

A new sport called MMA - Mixed Martial Arts - was starting to get some attention, and a company called UFC were bringing the show to Thailand.

Again, not really my thing, but as my finger hovered over the channel selector on the remote, I damn near dropped the thing when Brad's lovely face appeared less than half a metre in front of me!

He was now something of a celebrity, and as I watched his short interview, I felt a massive tingle down my spine as I noticed that my name was still tattooed on his arm!

His face looked a little rougher as I imagined the battles he had experienced since out last meeting. I cursed my luck for that night and the deceit that my once friend had planned behind my back.

The interview was brief but when he was asked about the name on his arm, I could see some regret in his eyes as he replied.

My English was still rubbish but the Thai subtitles were easy to follow:

'Whose name is that, Brad?'

He replied:

'A long-lost love of mine...'

This time, the remote did leave my hands and as the batteries were sent scattering across my hard floor, I felt a powerful pang of emotion.

The sports programme then switched to golf, so I turned it off manually and sat on the floor in a huge cloud of desolation.

'Ice, are you in?'

The loud voice of Dada and her customary three knocks on my door quickly brought me back to the present.

'*Nong-Sao*, whatever is the matter?'

As usual, my best friend was worried about me and this time, I couldn't hold back my emotions and tears. I poured out my regrets and even told Dada that I was still a virgin and how I wished I could get another chance to meet this beautiful man who was just in front of me, yet a million miles away.

She didn't say a word until I was spent.

Fixing me with her gorgeous smile, my 'big sister' simply replied:
'Okay, let's give this superstar one more chance...'

End of Chapter Six

CHAPTER SEVEN – SWEET AND SOUR

Buriram City

Ice

I had been working at Tawen Daeng for almost a year, and because I had lived frugally, my bank balance was looking good.

In my mind, I was soon going to return to the village on a break and see what was going on with the remains of my family. I hoped that Somchai had got his house in order, but I feared the absolute worst.

Had Mum returned or was she still gone? Shit, was she even alive?

I started to feel enormous pangs of guilt as I wondered about Nam and Oot, my younger siblings. To be honest, I was more confused than ever because I seemed to be the one who had walked out on them, not Mum.

Dada had advised me many times just to call them and see what was going on but when I tried, the number was unreachable.

'Ice, listen to me, you need them and they need you.'

She was correct, but it was pretty common here in Isaan for the eldest daughter to move away and start earning money for her family.

'Anyway, before you do this, let's reach out to Brad!'

She had a way of cheering me up that nobody else could, and as we sat down to create an Instagram account, I started to relax once more. This was nothing but a pipe dream but I was happy to play along as it appeared that Dada was quite the social media expert.

She used her laptop to set up my new account and we decided to use a photo of my tattoo as the profile photo, hoping this would somehow get his attention. I also found his Facebook fan page and posted my tattoo on there with a message.

This was merely some escapism for me, but it wasted a few hours, and I was amazed to see that he had over half a million followers on both platforms!

There was no way that he would see my message, and when Dada told me that most of the famous people have a minion to wade through the social media posts, I all but gave up any hope of connecting with Brad again. Instead, I was planning my return home, and was chuffed when Dada agreed to come with me, at least to have some back up if Aunt Peng was still around.

We both spoke to Pap and he allowed us two weeks holiday, unpaid of course.

Instead of attempting to connect to Oot or Nam on Facebook, I decided just turning up was better; after all, this was the Isaan way.

Dada had planned a big party for us at work, even though we'd only be away for a couple of weeks.

The next few days had passed by, and I had forgotten my pipe dream regarding Brad - at least the trip home was something to pass the time.

I withdrew most of my savings and was surprised at the weight of the envelope I was going to hand over to my family. Again, I wondered if Mum would return, but tried not to raise my hopes.

It would be a lie to say that I had enjoyed my first year away from home, but the cold hard facts were in that envelope.

Instead of working tonight, the ever kind Pap had given us the evening off, and this was on full pay! Our bags were packed, and we'd decided on splashing out on a taxi instead of dealing with the creaky old bus that stopped so many times.

We decided to start the evening off with drinks and food at one of Tawen Daeng's VIP tables and, for once, we declined offers from the male customers who seemed to be even more interested in the pair of us despite the jeans and T shirts we wore.

Eventually, as the drinks flowed, Dada convinced me to have a few more at the local nightclub before retiring for the night at my place. As we entered the club, I felt an involuntary shudder down my spine and wondered if this was such a good idea.

But after a few more drinks and some great live music, I soon forgot my worries and, as Dada pulled me up on my feet and over to the dancefloor, we started to have some serious fun.

'Work hard and play harder!

That was her mantra, but we must have only been dancing for at least 30 minutes when things started to go wrong.

Instead of having our own part of the floor area, people started to bump into us a little too often to be a coincidence.

Then I saw him.

Those unmistakeable features masked with a scowl.

It was Sombat…

The rest of the bullies were his friends from that night almost exactly one year earlier.

Dada tried to push her way through, but they were far stronger. I warned her to be careful.

'Dada, these are bad men, he is Nok's ex-boyfriend, the one I told you about before.'

After Nok had left town, I presumed he had followed her but that seemed not to be the case. They surrounded us and as Sombat leaned in, he whispered in my ear:

'Tonight is the night for revenge, you little whore!'

With that, they dragged us away from the dancefloor and towards the side door. I begged the security guards to help but they simply smirked and looked the other way.

'Don't ever fuck with Thai men like us, you will always lose in the end!'

I feared the worse as Dada was shoved to the floor and Sombat ordered his men to strip naked. He started groping me and forced his foul-tasting tongue into my mouth.

My eyes were closed as I braced myself for this most hideous of punishments. It seemed that when everything is going well, my life gets turned back on its sorry little head.

Just as I prepared for my impending sexual attack, I suddenly felt his body being pulled away and heard a painful yelp from my would-be rapist.

Then I heard a familiar voice and opened my eyes in disbelief:

'Hey little troublemaker, you still keeping bad company?'

Brad was stood in front of me and, as his friends beat the absolute shit out of Sombat and his henchmen, he leaned over and gave me a peck on the cheek.

'Excuse me one second, will you?'

He smashed his elbow into Sombat's nose as the thug tried to grab Brad from behind, I swear he didn't even move his perfect head.

'So, how are you?'

I was speechless and marvelled as these four men executed a very quick and potentially lethal set of moves on at least ten Thai men.

It was a mismatch by a long margin, and I would have bet my heavy envelope of money that Brad and his mates could have beat another 20 or 30 of these thugs with their skilful Mixed Martial Arts moves.

In less than a minute it was over.

When the three security guards approached, they asked me:

'Can you get his autograph please? He is the number one UFC fighter on the planet.'

Brad laughed and posed for a few selfies as the local police arrived. Some more selfies later, it became clear to me that it was just me left on the 'planet' that hadn't witnessed Brad's rise to the zenith of Muay Thai and MMA.

My hero superstar came back for me!

Dada was a little hurt, but she ignored my pleas to visit the hospital and invited our rescue squad back to her Mum's for noodles and whisky.

'I saw your post on my page and I just had to come and see you.'

Brad explained that he had never suspected me of being behind the first nightclub encounter, but he was worried that if we had become involved, his training schedule for the first fight would have been ruined.

I asked him what he meant, but he just pulled me closer and whispered:

'Because you are the most beautiful girl I have ever seen.'

This time he kissed me properly. His warm, full lips met mine at long last, and I nearly passed out, it was so damn hot.

We caught up with what we'd been doing since our last meeting, his recount took considerably longer than mine, as I was pretty much in the same situation as before.

'Ice, will you come with me to Bangkok?

I nodded excitedly, but then remembered my impending family visit.

Brad was keen to come along, so I spoke to Dada who was looking after the travel arrangements and she beamed her lovely smile as it appeared that one of Brad's friends, Phil, was also getting on rather well with her.

We crashed out on the floor and the next day, whilst collecting my travel bag, I got to know my saviour a little better. I was relieved to learn that Brad was only 21, just three years my senior, and that he was unattached in the girlfriend arena.

The year that had separated us was full of events for this superb athlete and his Thai, if anything, had improved leaps and bounds.

The four of us met up at Buriram bus station, mainly because Brad really wanted to experience the rural life and shunned the idea of using a taxi.

Dada almost ruined the mood by warning Brad and Phil about Sombat and his reputation:

'Be very careful with that man, he has killed before and will not let this slide.'

But they just laughed the threat off as if it was nothing.

The bus ride was as uncomfortable as ever, but made more bearable by Brad, as I was surprised to see how animated he was when taking in the Isaan countryside. It was as if he was drinking it all into his memory to be played back at another time.

Personally, I was a little terrified at the prospect of what was going on with my family. I'd had absolutely no contact with them, and silently prayed that things would be better than the shambles that I had left behind.

Brad had no idea about the state of my family, and I was also worried that whatever mess we found, would alter his perception of me, so when the bus rolled into my village, outside the 7-11, I was a bundle of nerves.

'Hey Ice, this place is so cool, thanks for allowing me and my homeboy to tag along!'

Brad and Phil were acting as if we had just landed on another world, perhaps they were right.

We all piled into the convenience store for some sorely needed cool drinks, and when I saw who was working behind the counter, I dropped my bag onto the floor in shock.

'Hey *pee-sao*,[1] what are you doing here?'

It was Oot and just along the counter I recognised the cute features of my other sibling, Nam!

I introduced them to Brad and Co and then felt a soft tap on my shoulder.

I swung around to see a middle-aged man, in a 7-11 uniform *waiing* me in respect.

It was Somchai!

It appeared that my entire family, apart from Mum, were running the local 7-11! This was the biggest and most pleasant surprise I could have received.

Although the shop was busy, the three of them managed to get a

---

1   *Pee-Sao – Big sister.*

quick short break, and Somchai handed over the keys to the house as he explained that Aunt Peng had long gone, and they decided to follow in my footsteps as soon as the jobs were advertised.

Between them, they earned some decent money and, as it was the school holidays, both of my sisters were contributing to our once failure of a family.

I was so pleased at this change in luck! As the four of us left them to finish their shift, Brad put his arm around me and gave my bum a little squeeze. Although public displays of affection were frowned up in villages like mine, I had never felt happier.

We reached my home and I was again pleasantly surprised to see a long-awaited improvement.

The noodle stall had been modernised - it looked as if the family had decided to open in the evenings, according to a smart sign, and… was that a Facebook logo at the bottom?

I invited Brad, Dad and Phil to take a seat outside and had a look in the kitchen to see if there were enough ingredients for some lunch. I was starving and wasted no time in finding a huge wok, coriander, fish sauce, noodles and some tasty-looking prawns.

Twenty minutes later, I served up a massive sharing bowl of steaming food to my guests, along with cold drinks and some cured pork I had found in the fridge.

Brad and Phil then made a quick trip to the 7-11 for beers and pretty soon we were having a little party of our own.

When Somchai and my sisters had finished their shift, we fired up the noodle shop and, probably thanks to the two handsome foreigners, half of the village rocked up to order their suppers.

I showed Brad how to prepare the food and was a little shocked when Phil started live streaming our activities to their UFC page.

'Oh my God! Ice, look at how many people are watching us right now!'

I looked at Dada's iPad and she was right! Over 50,000 views already, and a lot of positive comments were popping up. Brad was having a ball and even Somchai seemed to be making the most of this social media exposure.

I was shocked to see a humble Bot arrive in his old beat-up car, and it appeared that he and my stepdad had made up since their last scuffle.

After his old friend had left, I took the opportunity to ask him for a little chat. Inside the house and away from the crowd, I bowed to Somchai as I presented him with my envelope.

He was amazed and started crying as he counted the sizable sum inside.[2]

I swelled up with pride and told my step-dad how proud I was of the way he had turned things around. Somchai eventually stopped crying and asked me in a serious voice:

'How is your mother?'

This, I wasn't expecting. I shook my head and replied:

'Somchai, I haven't see her since she left last year.'

I saw a look of guilt shoot across his face and remembered that I was still out of the loop as to what happened the day she said goodbye to me.

He was hiding something, or at least he hadn't been entirely sure if I knew why Mum left so suddenly.

'Somchai, you need to be honest with me, please!'

The man in front of me seemed to crumble to the floor and he was prostrate at my feet as both his and my own tears returned. There was something terrible about this scene, and I found it hard to remain calm as he started to tell me the reason Mum had left and how she had come into that large sum of money.

Once he had finished, I had to walk away to process what I had just been told.

I could hear his voice behind me fading away:

'Please Ice, please forgive me and please ask her to come back...'

---

2   *In Thailand, it is customary to continue to support your family long after you leave home. The term 'Gat-dtan-yuu' is used to describe this commitment, literally translated as 'Debt of gratitude'.*

But how could I? Somchai had sold my Mother to his closest friend for the sum of fifty thousand baht. No wonder she had left us.

I felt such a surge of emotions that I couldn't speak.

I walked past the noodle stall and dozens of customers, friends and family.

Brad eventually noticed me walking in a weird state and caught up with me.

'Hey troublemaker, what's wrong?'

He took my hand and led me to the side of the house where the old swing chair was still located, and we sat down. I told him everything in a flood of emotions, it was as if I needed to expel the foul information as quickly as possible.

Then the tears came.

Brad just sat there quietly, and now it was his time to process the failings of my pathetic family from a year earlier. This would probably be enough to scare this gentle yet incredibly strong young man away forever.

Who could blame him?

Culture shock is one thing, but this dysfunctional family where husbands sell their wives to the highest, or only, bidder, well… those are the actions of a true low class bunch of losers.

Taking both of my hands, Brad gave the slightest hint of a grin and just said:

'Gee Ice, that is nothing, you should see my family back in the US, they are ten times worse.'

I looked into his eyes, unsure if he was just humouring me.

'Why the hell do you think I am on the other side of the globe, hey?'

He went on to talk about his own experiences and did a great job of making me feel better about my own.

'Sure, Somchai did a stupid thing, but maybe he was in a real bad place, and has certainly shown that he's a better person now. We should go and get your Mum as soon as we can!'

I shook my head in disbelief because this fighting superstar was winning my trust and my heart in so many ways.

Then I did something that I will never forget, so out of character but just so right.

I led him by the hand, through the back part of my home, up the stairs and into my bedroom. The same place where I used to fantasise about the other Brad since my early teens.

He could sense that despite how much I loved him, I was hesitant and unsure. My previous experiences tainted what should be an amazing milestone in a young woman's life, but I wanted this to be special, the good kind of special, for the both of us. As if he could read my thoughts, he stroked my cheeks and kissed me softly, but firmly.

He then took control and as I gave him my virginity, it was as if he knew exactly how to press my buttons, it was even better than my dreams. I had heard about orgasms, but never in my wildest dreams had they been so amazing as the multiple times I came with Brad inside me.

We lay there afterwards for about fifteen minutes and no words were spoken between us; they were not needed. I was now a woman and Brad was my man.

We spent the rest of the night in our arms after I briefly checked on the happenings outside and could see that Somchai was still sitting alone.

I couldn't bring myself to speak to him, not yet.

Despite feeling so horny, I didn't make love with Brad again that night but in the morning, I just couldn't help myself.

'Wow, Ice! You are certainly a fast learner!' he gasped after our morning bonding session.

He must have known that I was a sexual novice, but I had plans to get up to speed just as soon as we got to Bangkok.

We spent three more days with my family and Dada asked if she could come along for the ride with Phil and we were to stay at Brad's hospitality suite at the Oriental Hotel.

I couldn't believe how fast things had moved and had to literally pinch myself to see if this was just a beautiful huge dream that I was in.

But it was real.

With no plans to return to the Tawen Daeng, I spent some time wondering about my future and still really didn't know if Brad was a part of it, or if I was just another distraction for this famous young superstar?

The morning that we were leaving came around quickly, and it was as if Brad was having the same thought process as I was. He led me to the swing chair and looked at me with intent and asked me:

'Listen Ice, I don't know what happened to us yesterday, but I want to make my intentions known right now.'

He pulled me closer and kissed me full on the lips, then moved his mouth away just a tiny distance so we were almost touching but allowing him to continue speaking.

'I have no idea how these things work in your country, but I'm intending to spend the rest of my life with you, my little troublemaker!'

He went on to explain that, in a week, he was due to fly back to the US before embarking on a world tour with the UFC organisation. This was almost too much to take in, and he then put it out there:

'Ice, do you have a passport? I want you by my side, always!'

Of course I didn't have one, but I explained that I had my birth certificate, ID card and that should be enough to get the ball rolling at the Thai Embassy.

His handsome features lit up and we hugged for what felt like seconds but in fact we had to stop eventually as I felt eyes on us.

A familiar mocking voice ruined the moment:

'*Nong-Sao*, I thought you would wait for me?'

It was Bank and he had another man with him. They both looked like crap and I guess Brad could sense that these were not friends as he released me and turned to face the pair of miscreants. As they sloped off like the cowards they were, I wondered if it would always be this way when Thai men realised that they were second best?

Instead of using the bus, Brad insisted on arranging for an airport limousine to collect us and less than an hour later, we were waving goodbye to my family.

I had spoken again to Somchai and although he was unforgiven, I promised to bring Mum back to him and their two daughters.

I spent a few minutes with Nam and Oot and gave them instructions to call me immediately if Somchai started to lapse again. Their eyes lit up when I told them that Mum would be home, I just prayed that I could find her and convince her to do this.

Who knows what massive emotional wounds she was being forced to live with, maybe it was a step too far?

But I had Brad with me and even Dada insisted on coming down to Bangkok to help. I felt that, with this team, nothing was out of the question.

We waved goodbye, climbed into the huge limousine and headed towards Buriram city. I needed to stop by my apartment and get my documents and Dada needed to check on her mother before the airport.

Brad and Phil went with Dada as they wanted to say goodbye to her mum for the kindness she had shown them before.

I could hardly believe how perfect he was, and this was happening so fast that I needed to take a moment on my own before looking for my papers. Staring in the mirror, I couldn't for the life of me see what was remotely special about the girl in front of me for someone like Brad to offer her his heart.

I got myself together and winked at my reflection before the search for my birth certificate and a few other documents began.

Typically, it took a while, and I was so engrossed in my hunt that I hadn't noticed the two men who entered my tiny apartment.

I heard footsteps and as I turned my head, a hard object struck me on the side of my face and I was out for the count.

Sometime later, I was aware of noises and as I awoke, I could feel that my arms and legs were bound together. I looked up to see the vile features of Sombat and, to my surprise, Bank and the other guy I had seen in the village sneering down on me.

I was naked and it looked as if finally, these bastards were going to have their way with me. Trying to scream, I realised that my mouth was full of some kind of material that stunk of gas or oil.

The group high fived each other and started to undress in front of me:

'Okay, you stuck up 300-baht whore, this is where you finally understand what a lowlife you really are.'

Bank literally spat these words out and it looked as if he was going to be the first of these scumbags to defile me. They must have been waiting for me for hours, or even days, and I cursed my luck that I had to stop by for my papers.

Sombat was still clothed as he forced my legs apart, while Bank seemed to be preparing for this vile action.

Then I heard movement outside and I wondered how many other men were here to end my life?

The front door flew open and I could make out the features of Dada, with Brad right behind her.

The three Thai men looked shocked, and I breathed a massive sigh of relief as Phil climbed through the window and dragged Bank away from me.

Brad punched Sombat several times and he was finished before my hero had even broken sweat.

Bank left the room the same way Phil had entered, but he went head-first, and the side window seemed to have an issue with his face as glass met flesh with only one winner.

'Oh Ice, what have these pricks done to you?'

Dada was in tears as she tried to undo the knots. They were too tight for her, so Brad politely moved her aside and produced a small knife that did the trick.

I managed to remove the oily rag from my mouth and was

struggling to shout a warning as the third man appeared from his hiding place.

I was unable to make a sound quickly enough, as I noticed too late he was holding a revolver and pulled the trigger three times.

I closed my eyes briefly and then released the loudest scream from the bottom of my lungs as I witnessed Brad, Dada and Phil hit the floor in unison.

The man then aimed his gun at me, and I felt a sharp pain just before my mind registered the gunshot sound bursting through my ears.

***

Ice's Dream sequence

I opened my eyes with some trepidation to find myself back in my village, at home.

Somchai appeared much younger, and he was explaining about the way that things didn't always appear as they were.

My two younger sisters and I were sat on the floor, watching him in awe as he continued to talk, stirring away at a medium sized pot.

After focussing on the scene, I remembered how this played out.

The three of us were distraught when we were denied the ten-baht daily drink called Vitamilk. There was a mini scene because Somchai couldn't spare the thirty baht needed for this little treat.

We learnt late that he had lost his last 100 baht on a silly wager, typical of him really.

Upon arriving home, he had sat the miserable trio down and started heating up some water. To this, he added sticky rice and a small amount of honey. He had then removed the pot and retreated into the kitchen.

Returning triumphantly a few minutes later, Somchai had presented us each with a bottle of Vitamilk branded bottles each containing a slightly cloudy liquid.

'Now close your eyes and drink!'

He commanded with some vigour.

We did so and the contents did indeed taste like our lovely Vitamilk!

I remember this so well, and as I closed my eyes once more; I could taste that sweet and nutty flavour as if it were real.

***

'Ice, please open your eyes!'

I did so but found myself laid down in a bed and looked around my new surroundings.

The lady speaking so softly to me was a nurse and it was obvious that I was in hospital. She walked away, and I looked in vain a little closer to work out what was going on.

The rest of the day consisted of me being fed several times, and each time I asked about my friends, I was met with a blank stare and no reply. As the sun started to set, I felt a little stronger and, although my head was bandaged, it didn't hurt so much.

I recalled the terrible scene from my apartment and started to panic about the possibility that Brad may have been killed, as well as Dada and Phil.

There was a newspaper on the hospital bed table, and I managed to grab it without too much effort. I looked at the date and was shocked to realise that I must have been out for two days.

I then looked at the headlines and as I digested the words and what they meant, I dropped the newspaper on the floor and started to shake uncontrollably.

They read:

'*World champion fighter shot dead in Buriram along with two unnamed victims.*'

My world was in tatters and as I screamed out his name, the room started to fill with medical staff. The last thing I can remember seeing was a large needle being stabbed into my arm.

And then nothing…

End of Chapter Seven

PART III – THE BIG MANGO

CHAPTER EIGHT – NEON JUNGLE

Nana Plaza, Bangkok – One month later

Ice

'Come this way if you want to live, girl!'

The *farang* was screaming in my ear and pulled my arm so hard that I really had no choice. The funky smell of this place was both repulsive and at the same time strangely captivating.

I was being pushed into a small, dirty cupboard that looked to be outside a ladies' toilet, and those heady aromas were soon replaced by bleach and piss.

The tiny door was slammed shut and I was alone.

I could hear a commotion outside and lots of shouting, glasses breaking and girls screaming.

Terrified that the door would pop open and leave me exposed to the horror outside, I held my breath and said a prayer to Lord Buddha. If he was listening, I expect he would had looked on disapprovingly and muttered something about Karma.

But was that even fair?

Sure, I had created some drama in my time, but I was never the main protagonist, and trouble just seemed to have a way of knocking on my fucking door when least expected.

Whenever I was comfortable, shit would get real, and those I loved got hurt or even worse.

Brad, Dada and Phil were dead.

Yet here I was, alive and still being pursued by my real life demons.

I held back my tears and tried in vain to blot out those tender memories of the man who was going to change my life, my dreams, our future.

I could still smell his sweet skin and imagined his loving touch as we kissed for the last time the day before those fuckers shot him in cold blood.

I must have dozed off with those thoughts in my mind, because eventually the cacophony of noise outside my tiny safe place was replaced by the sound of nothingness.

But I couldn't dream anymore. They had been replaced with a dull void that pretty much summed up my life.

Hopes dashed and any chance of a future were smashed to pieces by those bullets that cut into Brad's body like he wasn't even there.

I opened my eyes again and tried to tune into what had happened.

I recalled being chased up hard stone stairs and around a kind of balcony filled with bright lights and packed with people. Many of them were girls just like me, but wearing heavy make-up, push up bras and lipstick shades that eclipsed the rainbows I used to love back in my home village.

Just as the group of men were on me, I took a left-hand diversion through a curtain and into an ice-cold interior that had ladies dancing around poles, most of them wearing nothing but birthday suits. When I saw one of them dancing with a huge snake tangling around her neck and limbs, I started to wonder if I was still in this word or a much more sinister place.

There were white faces everywhere, and one man was pawing at my flesh as if I were no more than a snack for him to devour.

I looked back at the entrance and with relief I noticed my pursuers were nowhere to be seen.

Taking my eye off the path, I ran straight into a *farang* who had the biggest smile I had ever witnessed.

'Welcome to Angel Witch my lovely, now get your beautiful arse in that cubby hole before those lunatics get past my men!' he said, as I went crashing to the ground, arse over tit.

∗∗∗

Much later, I was still in the cramped cupboard, and I reached out with all of my senses to try and fathom if I was safe or not.

The same voice was just about audible and getting gradually louder.

I tensed up as I waited for the inevitable opening of the door, clenching my teeth as my imminent exposure loomed.

'There she is!'

The *farang* was looking down on me, offering out his hand in a very gentle manner.

'Come on love, let's get you out of there and see what the hell has happened to you.'

I really had no other choice, but my pride still made me refuse his hand as I scrambled out and onto my feet.

The club was now empty, except for him and a few older women who were half-heartedly cleaning the place. The man held out his hand again, and one of the cleaners looked at me and rasped:

'Don't be a fucking idiot, this man is kind and will help you!'

I tried to push past her, but there was no space, so I resigned myself to whatever he had in store for me.

'My name is Dave. I just want to know what has happened to you?'

Accepting my fate, I followed him to a booth, where I was surprised to see three or four bowls of steaming Isaan food on the table.

'Tuck in lass and take your time, we'll make sure nothing bad happens, okay?'

Although I could hardly understand him, this man had a very gentle way about him, and despite my foolish pride, I was hardly in a position to argue. I took a spoon and started to taste the food; it was as delicious as I remembered it. The hot and sour soup was crammed with juicy prawns and cooked just the way Mum used to back in the village.

I was halfway through the second plate when he came back, this

161

time with a younger woman who was scowling a little at me in a mocking way.

'Mr David, he wants to know what trouble you are in.'

And then in a harder tone:

'If you are on drugs or in trouble with the police, you must fucking leave now!'

Dave looked shocked at this outburst and held up his hand to the younger woman whilst looking straight into my eyes:

'Darling, just tell me why you are here?'

In my best broken English and with half a mouth of sticky rice, I blurted out:

'I have come to find my Mother!'

He smiled, waved the other girl away, and left me to finish my food in peace.

***

Buriram Province - One month earlier

Bank

After Sombat had shot the two farang and the Thai girl, he dragged me and Somchai away from Ice's apartment and drove us about fifty kilometres away from Buriram. I was still reeling with shock; come to think of it, the last few weeks had just gone from bad to worse.

With that fucking lunatic Rambo gunning for us and now the double murder of two international sports heroes, we were well and truly fucked.

The only thing we could do to stand a hope of avoiding life imprisonment now was to ensure that Ice was taken out of the picture permanently.

As for Rambo, well… surely the three of us could deal with his arse later.

So when, four weeks later, one of our spies called us to say the luscious Ice was on the overnight bus to Bangkok, that was the light at the end of this hideous tunnel that might just save all three of us.

Somluk

Bank was right, we'd well and truly hit pay dirt when we heard that Ice was on the bus and we wasted no time in following the vehicle all the way to Bangkok.

There was no point taking her out earlier, because we had business in Krung Thep and could easily dispose of her dead body in some back street or smelly canal. I wasn't sure why Sombat wanted to come along, but I guess he still wanted revenge for that shit Ice had pulled with her American boyfriend and his buddy.

So what if they were famous athletes? This is Thailand, and they are just worthless *farangs*!

We still needed to face up to the fact we'd killed Rambo's little sister, and that meant kill or be killed.

As far as I knew, he was already asking questions about us, and it wouldn't be long before we were faced with his ugly face and that Desert Eagle he loves so much.

The one thing bringing me comfort was that Sombat was probably his physical equal, and I had a feeling that we'd be okay.

***

Sukhumvit Road, Bangkok

Sombat

I had already got sick of these two idiots whining and complaining, so when the bus finally pulled into Ekamai station, I was ready to shoot that little bitch Ice and leave them to their own devices.

I was heading for Pattaya as I knew Nok would be there.

The bus stopped and all of the passengers piled out, all except Ice. I climbed onto the steps and pulled my gun on the driver, telling him to get the fuck out of my face.

Scanning the rows of seats, I eventually spotted her. She must have seen us following and was huddled on the back seat trying to imitate a pile of clothes.

'I see you, bitch!'

The pile of clothes grew a head and started frantically hitting the large rear window.

I scoffed and moved towards her waving my pistol. Of course, I had no intention of killing her here, but I knew that I wouldn't get a better chance.

It only took seconds to reach her and I could sense a crowd gathering outside the bus. I leaned over to drag her back by her hair and got a mouthful of her trainers for my troubles.

This bitch was tough, and she nearly got past me, but a swift clunk of my trusty revolver behind her ear did the trick.

She hit the deck and less than a minute later, all four of us were in my car heading for Sukhumvit Road.

***

Nana Plaza, Bangkok

Ice

As I polished off the rest of the Isaan feast, I surveyed my surroundings and started to think about how I ended up here. This was a gogo bar, and although I had seen these before, it was my first time to actually see one up close.

It was pretty large, with plenty of seating space, and I imagined how it would transform as the day got cooler and the chairs would start to fill up with customers.

The photos on the walls told their own story of pretty girls dancing around the poles. All of the men in the photos looked old with grey or no hair; I wondered to myself if Ying or even Nok had been to this particular place.

My head hurt and I recalled how that bastard Sombat had knocked me senseless yesterday evening on the bus. I was lucky to be alive, and I doubted that I could remain this way for much longer.

My life was such a fucking mess right now and the only thing driving me on was the hope that I could find my mother here in Bangkok.

✳✳✳

Ice - *The previous evening*

After I woke up in Sombat's car, I couldn't move because one of the three men had bound my arms behind my back.

I looked across and recognised the scowling features of my neighbour Bank next to me.

'Oh you little bitch, you will be begging for mercy after I have finished with you!'

I just looked away, because he wasn't worth a reply. These scum couldn't possibly make me feel any worse.

They had blown away my dreams and my man four weeks earlier, so what else could they do?

I hadn't dared to return to my village after being released by the hospital, so of course they would be waiting for me.

Although I had never been to Bangkok, I looked out of the window at the passing city scenery and, despite my predicament, it really was quite the spectacle. Thousands of people walking along the endless sidewalk with their heads down, either coming home or on their way to work. Countless street food stalls playing host to the hungry citizens of this huge city.

Accepting my grisly fate, I yearned to taste those dishes that they took for granted and pondered about my next life: would I come back as a Bangkokian, or perhaps I was destined to be nothing more than a morsel being tossed in a wok before sliding down someone's throat?

I imagined the beauty of this city on a clear warm day and could almost imagine the sun bouncing off the pavement, as it was swatted away by commuters shielding themselves with yesterday's

165

newspapers.

'I want to fuck her!'

My sweet desperate evening dream was cruelly snatched away by Bank's words.

He started to lean over and squeezed my breasts as the others chuckled the way that men without any scruples tend to do.

'You horny little cockroach, we'll let you have her, but only once I've blown her little head off!' said the third man. I didn't know him, but he seemed to be the worst out of this malignant trio.

The car slowed and from the garbled conversation I gathered that the men had decided to stop for supplies. Pulling up on a garage forecourt, Sombat and the angry man leapt out and left me with my number one fan.

I could see just over the road, there were hundreds of bright lights and the thumping bass reminded me of the Tawen Daeng.

Surely there wasn't a branch here in the capital city?

'That's Nana Plaza!'

Bank was whispering in my ear, which was unfortunate, since his breath hadn't improved since the last time he tried to get personal with me.

His head was nuzzled in my chest and his left hand was pulling down my pants.

'Listen, if you want a good fuck, untie my hands and I'll get your cock hard!'

I could hardly believe the coarse language that was leaving my lips, but I knew that I had to do my best to copy what Ying would have done in this circumstance. She would surely have shot the little prick, but I didn't have that luxury, so I used what had.

Her words were still in my memory when I remembered that what I had between my legs was even more powerful.

He looked up and pulled a blade from his pocket saying:

'Finally, you have seen the light!'

It took seconds for him to slice the cable ties and his penis was out even quicker, he grabbed my head and forced it onto his erect member.

I tried not to gag as it was obvious this filthy scumbag had no idea of personal hygiene.

Taking him fully into my mouth, I bit down as hard as I could and almost gagged on the warm blood that was spraying down my throat and overflowing my mouth onto my face and clothes.

I wasn't sure if I had bit his manhood off completely but judging by the screams, it wasn't far off.

He reeled back and I took the chance to swing round and opened the door, thankfully they hadn't bothered to use the child locks.

I scrambled across the forecourt and could hear the other two men in pursuit, this was my only chance and I sprinted for my life, in every sense of the word.

Somluk

I could hardly believe my ears and ears as I saw the little slut run across the forecourt towards the Nana Plaza. Then I heard the screaming coming from the backseat of the car and slowed down just enough to see Bank covered in what I guess was his own blood.

His groin area was drenched, and I thought about stopping to help him, but what was the point?

Sombat had already overtaken me so I followed suit, and we ploughed through the huge crowd who were assembled around the entrance. We nearly lost her because there were just so many people, *farang* and Thai girls, that she all but disappeared from plain sight.

Sombat was about ten metres ahead of me and he started pointing to the stairs.

Sombat

That fucking waste of space had let Ice go, and it looked as if she was going to escape the more I shoved people out of the way in the packed Nana Plaza entrance area.

The air was hot and sweaty, and my rage was rising with every fat and old *farang* standing in my path. One of them actually took a clumsy swing at me, but I smashed him to the ground with my elbow and smirked as he went sprawling onto the tarmac.

By luck, I looked to my left, and could see her squeezing past bodies on the stairs that led to the upper levels of Nana Entertainment Plaza.

I should have shot her back by the bus, or maybe aimed properly back at her apartment a month earlier.

This whore appeared to have more lives than a cat, but surely this was her last dance.

Again, I had to contest with writhing bodies, it was so tempting just to remove my side arm and start blowing these old perverts away.

I felt a tap on my shoulder and saw Somluk breathing heavily as we reached the first floor. The human traffic was a little lighter here and we started to make up ground on Ice.

In fact, we almost ran past the bitch as we hit the corner bar, but there she was, briefly as she slipped through the velvet curtain, as if it were her first night at a new job.

David

It was a typical Friday night in Angel Witch gogo bar in Nana Entertainment Plaza. When I say typical, I mean absolutely anything could happen!

I am the manager of the best gogo bar in Bangkok, if not the world, and I absolutely love my fucking job! Surrounded by beautiful half naked girls and free booze all night, what is not to like, hey?

Right now, however, there is some kind of a disturbance at the entrance and even my tough security guards seem to be having issues dealing with it.

I made my way there and pushed past the closed thick curtains to see a pair of crazed looking Thai men waving guns in the air and looking menacingly at my poor security men.

'What the fuck is going on here?'

I half screamed and was surprised at how high my voice sounded. Park, my main guy, turned around and replied:

'Mr David, these two are Thai Mafia and they want to come inside.'

Typically, Thai men are not allowed in my club because they unsettle both my girls and the customers, but these were no ordinary men.

'They saw a girl come inside and they want to take her.'

Well, that settled it! There was no way these two wankers were going to have access to my girls. I instructed my men to hold them and turned on my heel to see if she was still inside.

I saw a beautiful Thai girl who was obviously running for her life and helped her into one of the lockers next to the toilets.

Thankfully, she was slim enough to fit inside, and once I locked her in, I returned to the fracas that was developing outside my club.

Eventually they fucked off, and the next morning we caught up after she stuffed her pretty face with some Isaan food my cleaning lady brought inside.

Present day

Ice

After eating my meal, Dave gave me some much-needed space, but about ten minutes later I felt the need to speak to him and asked the older cleaning lady if she could fetch her boss.

She scurried off to find him, not before she administered me a vile look.

Once he returned, I was surprised to learn he could speak Thai quite well and without his prompting, I told him my story, well at least from the part where Brad was killed and how his killers were now after me.

He smiled and asked the younger girl to call somebody.

'So Ice, what is it you plan to do now?'

He explained that it was far from certain that he could keep me safe, but that also he had no plans to turn me over to these dangerous thugs.

After making a few phone calls, Dave asked the younger girl to take me to the rooms upstairs. These were accessed without leaving the club, so I felt safe from my pursuers, at least for now.

'My name is Meow' the girl introduced herself, flashing a smile that disarmed me.

After I replied with my own name, Meow led me up the corridor and into a tiny room that was pretty much taken up by a huge unkempt mattress.

She asked me to relay the story her boss had been told about how I had appeared in the club that night, and I was only too happy to share.

Her face went ashen when I explained how my lover had been shot dead in front of me and then how I took a bullet as well. Eyes as wide as saucers, betraying no emotion, up until the part where I used my mouth to show how I had bitten down on Bank's penis.

Meow then erupted into a laughing fit so severe that I worried she would suffocate. Her noise was so loud that another three ladies from next door appeared and once she had recovered, I was made to repeat the story word for word.

One of the newcomers started to point at my shirt and screeched:

'Look! She still has the blood from his cock on her clothes!'

I looked down and, true to her word, there were large spots of blood all over my shirt.

I looked up again. I now had an audience of almost ten, and it was apparent that I had to tell my story all over again. I was paid in beer and more noodles for my efforts, and I guess it was a fast track into this beautiful gang of girls at Angel Witch.

About the fifth time into the story, I was interrupted by a shrill alarm and was surprised to see that my fan-club stood up and ran out of the tiny room.

Only Meow remained.

'Time for work!' she whispered.

I felt some inclusion in this group thanks to my dramatic reprisal of the last 24 hours of my life. Secretly relieved, I followed her out of the room and downstairs into the club.

Although it was barely the afternoon, the place seemed busy, and I took a seat to take in what was happening.

There were about five stages, each of them different sizes, and all with semi-naked girls parading their wares. I couldn't spot any that were less than stunning, and most seemed to be my age or just a few years older. Ying had once told me that *farangs* like them young, and she was already considered to be too old for places like this.

The music was so loud that I soon started to feel a little disorientated as the lights dimmed and customers started to arrive.

The familiar features of Dave were suddenly in front of me as he asked my age. He grinned with relief as he learned I was old enough to work in his club. I asked if I should climb onto the stage and he laughed back, mentioning something about me being a server.

'But what about those men from last night?' I asked with genuine concern.

He just laughed and instructed Meow to fetch me a server's vest.

Dave

She was a real cutie but way too young for me. I knew that she would probably end up being a dancer, but for tonight, I needed Ice to keep a low profile. Those mafia wankers would be back, I'd lived in Bangkok long enough to know their type.

I had a contact down in Pattaya who I could call on to deal with this type of scum. He was a real hard case, not to be messed with and he owed me one after I gave his cousin a job as one of my dancers.

We get all kinds of famous people in here, and even Steven Tyler from Aerosmith would pop in whenever he was in the area.

Anyway, back to this fellow I know, he seemed a little distracted on the phone, as it appeared he was on a manhunt of his own. One of his family had been killed and he was heading up North where they had last been seen. Then he asked about the incident and if I had any footage of the pair of thugs.

As it happened, I did, because the club has state-of-the-art surveillance equipment, and both of their ugly mugs were caught on camera.

I sent the video files down to him but heard nothing back. Kind of put a damper on the evening as I wondered just how badly they wanted little Ice.

I warned my guys and they managed to get a few extra lads to back them up if, or more like when, it would all kick off later.

The rest of the afternoon was without incident and Ice seemed to take to her new job like she was born to it.

Somluk

I made a note to give that *farang* wanker a proper kicking tonight and tried to hold back a giggle as I listened to Bank groaning every time he bent over.

Ice had taken a nice chunk out of his cock, but the doctor had managed to re-attach it. He was on enough pills to stop an elephant and was hell-bent on snuffing her out his time.

I didn't care who killed her, but she needed to leave this world tonight by any means necessary.

Bank

We approached the Nana Plaza and I could still feel that bitch chomping down on me as I was just a snack for her to devour.

Who would have thought that little Ice from next door would transform into such a hard bitch?

Sombat

This time would be different, we knew there were men on the door but they were just rented muscle, not real mafia like I was.

As for my two accomplices, this would be the last time we would work together. Since that chance meeting back in Buriram, they had done nothing but slow me down.

Yes, once Ice was done for I thought I'd drive a few hours down South and see where Nok was hiding these days. No doubt she would be waiting with open legs and a smile as wide as Sukhumvit Road.

We reached the door to the club and I was dismayed to see the front of house had doubled up, but once I pulled out my sorn off shotgun, that number dwindled to zero as they sloped off, suddenly losing interest.

The three of us were inside and I blew a cartridge into the ceiling by way of announcing our arrival.

Dave

Fucking hell, they were back and this time armed to the teeth!

I first looked at them and then checked to see where Ice was, but she was either hiding or had legged it, both good survival choices.

The three armed men marched up to me. It was time to see what I was made of once more.

I signalled for the DJ to turn off the music and shouted out for the dancers and servers to get out of sight, the last thing I needed was a bloodbath.

The craziest looking one thrust his pistol flush to my forehead and started shouting in broken English:

'You want die, *farang*?!'

'Not really, mate' I replied, noticing a scuffle behind me as the other two wankers rushed past.

It was apparent that they had spotted Ice.

Turning back to me, the gunman rasped:

'We kill her then we kill you, arsehole!'

Now, normally I would be absolutely bricking myself but, you see, I had a trump card. Just on cue, he appeared at the entrance holding a great big fucking machine gun.

I shit you not, at that split second, the music started blaring through the Angel Witch's powerful speaker system, and even the fucking dry ice started to appear.

The song?

It was 'My Hero' by the Foo Fighters, as I live and breathe.

My buddy, Rambo, was here!

Somluk

We forced our way into the gogo bar, feeling good as I was holding the pump action shotgun. All of the girls were running for their lives and I followed Sombat right towards the pale-faced manager. Not kidding, he looked a little scared and even though he wasn't on my kill list, I really wanted to give the little shit a beating.

Then Sombat spotted Ice.

The other whores were trying to shield her from us. How sweet of them! Too bad she was going to die regardless.

We shoved past the manager, but then just as we were about to reach the slut from Buriram, I heard a voice that made my blood curdle.

'Hello Sombat, it's time to pay the piper!'

174

I turned on the spot just to be sure.

There he was, holding a fucking huge machine gun and smiling from ear to ear.

It was Rambo!

Rambo

Ever since I got that text with the photo of my dead sister, I have dreamt of the time when I could kill those Chicken Farm Crew fuckers. Turns out I was too late for Kwan, but now I was in the same club as Somluk, and revenge was going to be so very sweet.

My *farang* buddy Dave called me for some help, and when I saw who the protagonists were, I could hardly believe my eyes!

Knowing there were two other men with Somluk, I brought my favourite machine gun, as well as my Desert Eagle and a few other surprises.

Wannee allowed me to take some time off as I told her there was a funeral in Bangkok, I didn't explain that I was the one providing the bodies.

Dave dropped to the floor, so I had a clear shot on Somluk and sprayed a burst of bullets in his direction.

He caught most of them in his big head, and it was goodnight from that arsehole.

The mouthy one next to Dave started shooting at me, however not before I pulled my Desert Eagle out and blew his head clean off, almost perfect!

The third man who had a limp was trying to escape, and he would have nearly made it, had it not been for a few of the girls that blocked his path and one of them, a real beauty, drop-kicked him in the balls and he sank to his knees.

I dragged him out by his hair and just threw him over the balcony, he died instantly as he landed on his neck with a sickening crunch.

I would have loved to stay for a drink and a catch up with Khun Dave, but it made sense to walk away at that point.

I gave him a nod and jogged through the crowd, happy that I had evened the score and rid the world of three absolute wankers.

Dave

That will go down as one of the most exciting minutes of my life! That was how quickly the three stooges were wiped out by Rambo.

Checking my watch, it was getting close to the happy hour, so I asked the girls to help clean up the blood and, with the help of my guys, dragged the two remaining bodies out to the back of the club for disposal later.

Ice was long gone and, although I liked her, it was probably for the best.

Running one of the best gogo bars in Bangkok is hard work, but it is never dull!

End of Chapter 8

CHAPTER NINE – ON NUT AND MAE NAK

Sukhumvit Road, Bangkok – One hour later

Ice

I seized the chance to up and leave the terrible scenes in Angel Witch and never looked back.

Stupidly, I had left my suitcase back on the bus in Ekamai station, and that really pissed me off. I knew I had a good reason for it because those three hoodlums had dragged me off the bloody thing and I could hardly ask them to wait for me to disembark, but it was inconvenient, nonetheless.

I had a rough idea that I was on Sukhumvit Road and that Ekamai was also on this monstrous carriageway. More importantly, On Nut district was also somewhere off this huge structure.

We were taught back in school that Sukhumvit Road is actually the longest in the world, and you can drive all the way from Bangkok to Cambodia. Right now, I would have gladly walked there and back if it meant finding my Mother.

I missed her so much, and I really needed someone to hold me and make sense of the shit storm that my life had become.

I had witnessed more killings in the last month than I could count, and although some of them may have been deserved, I doubted that I would ever get over the stress and heartbreak my short life had been forced to endure.

The lives of a good friend and my lover had been snuffed out by vengeful men, and they in turn were now removed from this mortal coil.

What, or who, was next?

My time in Bangkok had been short but far from sweet, and my mind and senses were scrambled beyond belief.

What could I expect, even if I managed to find my Mother? Did she have some kind of magical fucking wand that would make everything alright again?

For all I knew, she could also be dead, and nothing would really surprise me anymore.

Sukhumvit Road was indeed immense, and I started to count the Sois to my left as a way to try and mark some kind of progress in this seemingly impossible journey.

I thought back to the club and the kind *farang* manager who had somehow summoned a demon with a machine gun from nowhere. This mythical beast had slain all three of my would be killers.

I wondered if I would eventually be working in such an establishment? Even though I enjoyed my time at Tawen Daeng, I could sense this was on another level.

As I passed the very same food stalls as yesterday, albeit in vastly different circumstances, I still felt like an outsider looking into a different world. Unlike the more casual set ups in the village, the hawkers were not smiling and seemed to even resent my hungry looks.

I had no money, and all of my possessions were in my bag that had been stowed on the bus. My only real hope was to somehow find that backpack, and even then, only if the money and clothes were still intact.

I purposely kept my shooting incident from my family as I suspected the perps would be close by. They were dead, but how would I know if they had told others about the incident? I couldn't even phone them now, as my mobile was in the fucking backpack as well.

I could see the sign for Ekamai, but I was miles away, as I knew it was near Soi 40 and I wasn't even near Soi 20.

My stomach was growling, and I was so thirsty that I contemplated grabbing a half empty bottle of water from a vacant table.

I was running on empty and had no idea what to expect.

The sweat was running into my eyes and the number of pedestrians seemed to double as the street stalls were on both sides of the pavement offering shirts and various merchandise to what looked like foreign tourists.

Any other time and I would have been engrossed by this scene as I love any kind of shopping spectacle, but today I was annoyed because this was slowing me down and I wasn't sure how much I had left in the tank. I had to literally pick my way through the throng, eventually having to stop as a large white lady blocked my path.

I was just about to tap her on the shoulder when I noticed a wiry man push into her from the opposite side.

He was like a human eel as I witnessed his bony hand somehow slip into her large handbag and back out again with an expensive looking purse.

Our eyes locked as he then swerved passed her and tried to shove me out of the way.

She hadn't noticed and I decided there and then to stop this thief with whatever means necessary. After all, I had been shot, twice nearly raped and kidnapped all in the last four weeks so what did I have to lose?

I grabbed at the purse and managed to trip him up with a move that dear Brad had shown me back in my village. He struggled briefly, and soon we were both on the ground wrestling over the lady's property.

'Stop, thieves! They are stealing my purse!'

The lady was screaming at the top of her lungs and this made her would-be thief jump up and run.

I got to my feet and handed her purse back. For a split second, it looked as if the stupid woman thought I was the one who was stealing. Thankfully, another *farang* explained that he had seen everything and it was in fact me who had saved her from being robbed.

A few minutes later and 500 baht richer, I managed to find a food stall and spent at least half of my winnings on some much needed food and water. Reflecting on my good fortune, I chuckled inwardly as I tried to avoid thinking too much at this time.

Feeling refreshed, I decided to continue walking to Ekamai rather than spend money on the BTS Skytrain. Eventually I arrived at the bus station and went straight to the office to see if my backpack was there.

The office worker was disinterested and shuffled off to get a form for me to fill in. I had no phone number and no address, so I was sure that this was just a waste of my time.

As I was just about to leave this dreary place, I walked towards the main road, wondering how my luck could get any worse, when I noticed a blue backpack just laying on a pair of plastic benched, right in the middle.

At this point I wasn't sure if it were mine or not, but there was nobody around so I just casually grabbed it and carried on towards On Nut.

About ten minutes later I crouched down, popped the top of the bag open and looked inside.

It was my bag!

Unbelievably, it was untouched and my money, phone and a few sentimental items were still intact.

Tears were streaming down my face and I felt I had to sit down, albeit on the dirty crowded pavement, in order to take this all in.

'Are you alright, Miss?'

I looked up to see an older man looking down and offering his hand.

Smiling, I waved him away, as I had no intention sharing my woes with anybody right now. My trust level was lower than zero and for good reason.

As I continued walking, I noticed signs for On Nut appearing on the overhead bridges. The pedestrian traffic had all but disappeared, and my resolve started to return.

The shops seemed to have transformed from fast food joints to more traditional Thai structures, such as hardware outlets and chemists.

After I took a right turn, I found myself in Soi 77, which was quite possibly the most interesting part of Bangkok so far. Street markets all but ran amok across this leafy street, and the place was so full of life I had to stop myself from reaching out to these cheerful people.

I made a pact to myself and my family that, since Brad's demise, I would think twice before speaking to any stranger, whatever their nationality.

The Isaan accent was prevalent amongst these shoppers and hawkers, and I was eventually to learn that most of these had moved to the capital in order to offer their domestic services to the Hi So people in neighbouring Thong Lor District.

Where Soi 77 met Soi 7, I was astounded to see a stunning temple known as Wat Mahabute. I was forced to stop to drink in the sheer beauty of this structure and then I noticed something that made me feel closer to my Mother than ever.

This was the place where Thailand's most revered ghost was allegedly laid to rest, Mae Nak.

Although I felt this wasn't the right time for a visit, I made a solid *wai* to the temple and crossed the street for some noodles and a much-required think. I recalled the many times that my Mother had told me of the tragic tale of the young wife who died in childbirth whilst her man was fighting for our country.

The similarities with her and my own Mother's fate seemed to be intertwined. The fact that my Mother survived but her soldier, my father, perished, still stayed deep within my core.

I fished out my phone and thankfully it still held a small charge. Calling my family for the first time since my shooting, I wept as I could hear the relief in their collective voices.

They had heard about the event but weren't sure that it was me. Foolishly, I never returned my sisters' calls, and had neglected to share my address in Buriram.

'Where are you now?'

Somchai sounded concerned but I could sense there was something else he wanted to tell me.

'I am in On Nut; I am looking for Mother…'

He started to cry and laugh at the same time. Before I could ask what was happening, another voice started speaking to me.

'Hello, my brave Ice, I am here back with Somchai and your sisters.'

After picking my phone up, cracked screen and all, I also started to make the deranged noise and more than one person looked my way with inquisitive looks.

So it transpired that my trip to Bangkok was a waste of time.

Or was it?

Once I had caught up with my Mother's last twelve months, I was overjoyed to learn that she was now at peace and had returned to her loving family. Somehow, she had forgiven Somchai and all was well with their relationship.

So I was now faced with a few choices: return to my village, go back to Buriram and Tawen Daeng, or something else entirely.

Thinking hard and trying not to take the easy option, I had almost made up my mind when my phone started to ring again.

Fully expecting to hear a family voice, I was shocked when the less familiar tones of Ying all but shattered my temporary peaceful state of mind.

'Ice! Is that you?'

I replied in the affirmative.

'Please, can you come now?! Your friend Nok is missing, and we need your help!'

I could hardly believe it, my so-called friend who had left me in the shit was somehow thinking I was interested in her wellbeing.

Maybe a year ago I would have dropped everything and done her bidding, but right now I couldn't care any less.

'Ice, are you listening?'

I could sense a lot of stress in Ying's voice, something I hadn't heard ever before.

'Yes, where are you?'

Her reply shouldn't have shocked me, but for some unknown reason, it resonated deep inside and I knew as soon as I heard that word, I had no fucking choice.

I was going to Pattaya.

End of Chapter 9

PART FOUR – MY DESTINY

CHAPTER TEN — PATTAYA, FINALLY

Ekamai Station, Bangkok

Ice

I was surprised to learn that the next two buses to Pattaya were full up and the last one of the day was also looking pretty packed. It seemed that ninety percent of the passengers were ladies between the ages of 18 and 30, and I was under no illusions about their reasons for making the trip.

Having waited three hours, I decided to push my way past the stragglers and squeezed into the sweaty interior amidst groans and cursing:

'Fuck your mother, you Isaan whore, I was next!'

Usually I would either apologise or have a go back at them, but right now I was just intent on staying on the damn bus. I counted at least twenty of us standing up and all of the seats were taken with tired bodies and all kinds of luggage.

I felt eyes on me and looked to my left where a middle aged woman seemed to be giving me the once over as if I was in a shop window.

'Hey cutie, I have a seat just for you!'

I looked down again and she had moved her belongings onto her lap, patting the empty space with some vigour.

'It's a long journey and you look in need of some food.'

Well, this was a surprise! I had heard the bus from Bangkok to Pattaya was a hideous experience with all kinds of detritus making the voyage. Perhaps it wasn't so bad after all?

I smiled sweetly and sat my sore backside down onto the hard seat, at least my poor legs would get some relief.

'Here, have some of this!'

A plate of noodles was shoved under my nose and I had to agree that these smelt really nice.

'So, honey, what is your name and where are you going?'

This one was persistent, and I already suspected that she had an ulterior motive for her onset of hospitality, but I really didn't give a shit as I was hungry.

'I am Ice from Buriram and I am going to see my friend.'

This seemed to tickle the lady as she replied:

'Oh, I am a Buriram girl as well, and I could tell you were from that part of Isaan, how exciting!'

I grinned back and started making serious inroads to the noodles, they were damn good!

After I had finished she took the bowl away and asked me about my plans once more. I tried to feign disinterest, but she kept pressing. She placed her hand on my cheek as if to get a better look of my face, making me reluctantly turn my head and flash her a killer smile.

This seemed to delight my mysterious benefactor as she asked:

'Ice, my dear, I have a proposition for you, why not come and work for me?'

I grinned in an attempt to buy some time to think of an excuse - I really had other things to do, like finding my friend Nok.

She handed me a smart-looking card and I read the name embossed in deep blue:

> '*Wannee – Club and Bar Owner – Pattaya and Bangkok*'

I looked again at her 'crocodile' smile as she squeezed my thigh, and involuntarily shuddered as a sixth sense started to tell me that she was very bad news indeed.

∗∗∗

Buriram Province
A few days earlier

Ying

I was back in my village for a rare trip to see my family when I noticed the small holdall that had been stowed away in the ramshackle shed behind the kitchen. I guess I was looking for nothing in particular when I came across the non-descript luggage item.

Thumbing through the contents, I was about to lose interest when a small plastic device fell onto the concrete floor with a dull thud.

Later that evening, I inserted the usb drive into my laptop and fully expected to see some boring temples or waterfall snaps that John used to spend his time recording with his expensive camera.

But these were nothing of the sort.

I did a double take when I first saw the image of the girl.

She was about nine years old. Naked as the day she was born and with a man who looked very much like my ex-husband.

Then it dawned on me.

John was a paedophile.

It took a good ten minutes to get over this hideous fact and then I retired to my old bedroom to check out the rest of the disgusting images.

There were thousands of photos and even some short movies.

I cried myself to sleep, weighed on heavily by the thought that the same hands that had ruined these young lives had also touched me all over.

The next day, I took the family motorbike and rode for about fifty kilometres to help me to see things on an even keel. This monster had not only tried to ruin me and my family, but he had committed acts against the human race.

He had to pay for this.

He had to die!

But then I weighed up the options. He was rich after all.

I hatched a plan whereby I would extract all of his money. I would make him beg for mercy. I would castrate this fucking human stain.

Then, and only then, I would hand him over to the police.

He would serve time in one of the worst prisons on the planet. Not a soft option back in England, no - he would go to Bang Kwan, here, in Thailand.

I would pay heavily to ensure this was the case.

Picking up my phone, I forwarded one of the images I had copied earlier and sent it directly to John's number.

I was sure it was still the same, because he was clumsy and careless, otherwise I would have never found these filthy images in the first place. These type of predators would eventually trap themselves, as they believed they were beyond the law.

That was what I had read before, and here was John, true to type.

I cried my heart out on the way back to the village, recalling how many of my school friends had met the same fate for their uncles, fathers and other male family members.

Thankfully, my own family had not messed with my childhood.

But was this normal or was I just lucky?

I hated men, and now I had even more reason to.

As I parked the bike up, my phone started buzzing and I read the reply to my opening gambit.

It read:

'How much do you want?'

That fat fuck had no idea that I was going to take everything he had and then some.

Sihanoukville, Cambodia

John

For the last year, I've lived the life of my dreams, and my two clubs are pretty much the best of their kind. I cater for a select audience and I know exactly what they like. Boi is still my right hand man and I pay him well for his expertise. He helped me to find these locations and then went the extra mile to fill the two places with quality merchandise.

Of course, I am talking about girls, but not just any old sluts. Not the rough old slappers you can find back in Pattaya or Bangkok, no, these are young and ripe and just what I needed to get the perverts from Europe and USA to come over in droves. I even put on a flight and hotel service for them, which also makes me a few coins to boot.

I had all but forgotten about that stupid bitch Ying and had no intentions of going back to Nakhon Nowhere, not now, not ever. She did well out of me, but thanks to my Bitcoin investment, I was still riding high as a crypto millionaire.

So when I got that email from her, it ruined my fucking day.

I couldn't believe how sloppy I had been.

I'd forgotten that the sodding USB drive existed.

How stupid was I?

She found it alright, and being a nosy little cunt, she wasted no time in checking out the contents.

Hundreds, if not thousands of photos, that I had amassed over the decades. All of underage subjects, and probably adding up to life imprisonment for yours truly.

She wanted money, lots of it. If that was the end of it, I wouldn't have minded, but I just knew that she would still probably stitch me up.

So here we were, Boi and I, on our way to Pattaya with one mission on our minds.

Find and kill Ying and destroy that fucking USB.

∗∗∗

Eastern seaboard of Thailand
12 hours later

Boi

So John and I were less than an hour away from the bright lights of Pattaya, and I must admit that I felt the buzz of nostalgia as I was reminded that this was the place I had so much fun. Wall to wall pussy, drugs, gambling - all on a quiet day.

Cambodia was okay, but Thailand was my home.

I had seldom cast my mind back to the lady who I had once loved, because there had been dozens more since.

But she was pretty special, this I had to admit.

Did I miss Ying?

Possibly.

Did I feel bad about leaving her?

Maybe.

Would I go back to her?

Not likely!

I was now richer than I had imagined, and although John was too much of a weirdo for my somewhat catholic tastes, he wasn't too bad.

As well as running one of his clubs, I was in charge of the gang who would roam the backwater towns of this backwards country, looking for teenagers to lure to their pretty limited futures working for John.

He would fly in dozens of similar types to molest these poor bitches, and so long as the local cops were paid on time, we never had so much as a parking ticket to worry about.

Occasionally, one of the workers would slit their wrists in an attempt to leave this terrible world, but we'd just pop back to the village they were spawned and grab a few more of the same, made no odds to us.

I had agreed to come along and get this USB drive back from my former lover but wasn't overkeen on snuffing her life out.

I even considered switching sides if the money was right, but I had a feeling that Ying had wised up in the last year. My friends in Pattaya told me that she now ran three clubs and was doing well.

With mixed feelings, I gunned the pickup truck down the Sukhumvit road and felt a distinct lump in my pants as the neon lights of Jomtien appeared on the horizon.

The fat fuck was snoring in the back seat liked a punctured toad, so I cranked the music up as I did what I had done for the last ten years.

I weighed up my options…

***

Chonburi, Central Thailand

Wannee

Buddha must have been smiling down on me when I decided to board the bus from Bangkok back to Pattaya. Usually, I will either drive myself or get one of my staff to do this, but for some reason Rambo was not available.

Sentimental idiot has not been the same since those fools accidently wacked his sister. I got a text earlier saying he had found them and avenged her, so hopefully he will be back up to speed soon.

Anyway, I digress. When that beautiful young North-Eastern girl shuffled along the bus queue and stopped next to me, I said a silent prayer.

She was exactly what my client needed.

Very pretty and with a great little body, but also an attitude that separated her from the other farm fresh bitches. In fact, I would have persuaded her to come and work in my bar, genuinely, but this was a different remit.

My client over in China had a specific line of business.

He was a snuff movie mogul.

Ice

This woman was very insistent, but my subconscious told me not to trust a word that came from her mouth. She was playing with her phone, and I swear that I caught her taking a photo of me - what the actual fuck?

Maybe a year ago I would have been naive enough to fall for her patter, but I was on this bus to Pattaya to help Nok and not one single thing would get in my way.

After I learnt that my family were complete once more, I was even more determined to put things right with the world.

Wannee, or whatever her name was, offered me a drink, only to seem really offended when I simply pointed to my bottle of water.

Did she think I was born yesterday? Even my Mother had warned me never to accept a drink or food from a stranger, especially on such a notorious journey as this one.

I really had no idea what to expect, and as I saw the bright lights getting closer and the bus pulling into Pattaya station, my stomach was in knots.

I tried in vain to get off the vehicle before this pushy bitch could feature me in her plans, but as I jumped off the bus, she was literally grabbing my shirt and impeding my ability to sprint off. I had no choice but to elbow her in the face in order to get free.

I had Brad to thank for that slick move, but it was all in vain. As I broke free, I ran straight into a man mountain and bounced onto the floor.

It seemed my plans were dashed once more.

I cursed the fact I wasn't a man and just a small weak girl.

Wannee

Ungrateful little bitch!

First, she refuses my sedative-laced drink, and now I have to deal with a lost tooth and a mouthful of blood. Oh, I was so determined that she would pay the price… I would be killing her myself if the Chinese customer had second thoughts.

As it was, he saw the snap I took, and said yes immediately. We'd smuggle her out via the North of Thailand in a truck, and two days later she'd be chopped to bits in the garbage skip, having had a fleeting moment as a doomed movie star.

That bony elbow really hurt. The only thing that helped with the pain was when I saw her literally run into the arms of Rambo.

He picked her up like the rag doll she was and hoisted her over his shoulder with a big soppy grin.

I needed to sort out my face, quite literally, so instructed him to wait for me by his car as I staggered towards the restrooms. It took a bit longer than expected as I needed shit-loads of foundation, as well as dealing with the blood stains on my shirt. That wretch certainly knew how to dish out an elbow.

About 30 minutes later, I found Rambo who was smoking a cigar, sat on the bonnet of his car.

I couldn't see the girl and was worried that he'd already killed her, especially if she tried a similar move on him.

'Where is she?'

He looked up and I noticed blood streaming from his nose.

'She's gone boss, that girl kicked me in the face and ran off like a little rat!'

I could have shot him on the spot, what the actual fuck had just happened?

Just as I was about to let loose, my phone started ringing and the name Boi flashed up on the screen.

What the hell was it now?

Rambo

Well I had literally just got back from the gun fight in Nana Plaza when Wannee's text, demanding my presence at the bus station appeared on my phone.

This was the last thing I needed, but she mentioned a large bonus if we got her latest target back in one piece, so I decided to make the short trip from my home in Jomtien.

The place was swelteringly hot despite the fact it was well after midnight and I stood outside the bus parking space as it rolled into view, packed to the brim with Isaan bitches. I sighed as I got ready to do what I do best.

I had to stifle a laugh as the target smashed Wannee directly in her face and had to alter my stance as she ran directly into my chest. Poor thing was half knocked out herself, so I hoisted her pretty arse over my shoulder and went back to my truck as instructed by a dishevelled and bloody looking Wannee.

I was only when I sat her on the bonnet that I realised that this was the girl from yesterday in Nana Plaza. The one who made Dave call me and led to the showdown that allowed me to avenge my dear sister's death in such a righteous fashion.

Although I had no idea what Wannee had in mind, I was certain that it was going to lead to her death.

She didn't actually recognise me and when I told her to punch me in the face, she looked as if I was bat-shit crazy.

I believe in Karma, and there was no way I could allow her to follow the path to doom that Wannee had already mapped out. I explained about how I knew her and she smiled sweetly before smashing me in the face with some force.

Whoever had taught her that move was worthy of my respect.

I had to put up with Wannee screaming in my ear for about ten minutes and eventually, after she calmed down, I drove her home in complete silence.

Walking Street, South Pattaya

Ying

I had not even begun my plans for John's demise when I heard his obnoxious voice downstairs.

How the fuck did he know where I was?

Somehow I suspected that old bitch Wannee was helping him, especially if it concerned getting one over on me and making a few million baht to boot.

John had lied to me when he said he'd be around next week, but that was no surprise given his track record.

When I made my entrance at the front of the bar, I was disgusted to see that the little fuckwit Boi was also in town.

Grinning from ear to ear, I had waited a long time for this moment.

I made a fake *wai* to John, walked past him and kicked Boi directly in the nut sack, thoroughly enjoying watching him fall down like the worthless piece of garbage he turned out to be. Unleashing a cigarette fuelled steam of phlegm on his neck, I turned back to John and asked him:

'So how much are you going to pay me for your private collection of underage girlfriends, you sick fuck?'

Instead of replying with a figure, he simply grinned and handed over his phone.

I could see a photo of my best friend on the screen.

It was Nok.

John

Ying was many things, but clever wasn't one of them. I had always been a few steps ahead of her and this was no exception.

I got Boi to call his contact in Pattaya, some pimp called Wannee, to let her know we were coming to town. She was a useful contact, as she even had some clubs in Cambodia and had sorted out a few issues for us before.

Boi explained that we had a problem with Ying and needed some leverage, for which, of course, she would be compensated. She advised us to grab some whore called Nok with whom, for some reason, Ying had struck up a relationship.

These bar girls seem to change like the wind, so Ying was now a lesbian? Nevertheless, that worked out just fine for me.

Wannee agreed to get one of her men to snatch Nok, and now here I was, in front of Ying, with the evidence that put the ball back in her court. Of course I was shitting bricks when I realised that she had the USB that could blow my world apart, but did I crack?

Absolutely fucking not.

I had to subdue a giggle when she floored Boi and was somewhat shocked when he later returned the favour with a right hook that sent her flying across the bar.

She was sobbing her heart out when we left and had nobody but herself to blame.

Still looked good though.

***

Second Road, North Pattaya

Ice

I had tried calling Ying about twenty times until I decided just to text her with my location and sit and wait. I found a quiet coffee shop and sat by the window facing the street, as I wasn't sure if that bitch Wannee would come back for second helpings.

Although my life had been a disaster since leaving the village, I always seemed to get through relatively unharmed.

Well, apart from a bullet and the odd rape attempt, I was still here and growing a thicker second skin that seemed to be shielding me from even worse possibilities.

Why I would even give a shit about Nok after she had left me was a puzzling matter, but I guess I was just a nice person.

Having found myself here in Pattaya for a good few hours, I was a little disappointed after hearing so much about this mythical place. To be fair, it was now the morning, and the bars and pavements were pretty deserted.

After being let go by Rambo, I spent the night on the beach, although I couldn't sleep. There were dozens of homeless people who made me really fear for my life, as my money and things were probably enough to secure me a ticket to the next world if the wrong person crossed my path.

Eventually, after my third coffee, my text got a reply, and I paid up before hailing a motorcycle taxi.

The address was in Jomtien Beach and I felt relieved to see Ying waiting for me outside what I presumed was her residence.

She looked terrible and as she hobbled towards the open gate, I felt a little hurt that she couldn't be bothered to even say hello.

I followed her into the house and, as she went to make me a drink I was shocked to see that the room had many photos of her and Nok together.

Ying returned with a glass of ice water for me and beckoned for me to sit down.

It was clear that she had a lot to say and I was all ears.

***

Ying

I had to explain to Ice how Nok and I had become lovers. Maybe it wasn't the most pressing part of us catching up, but it helped to remind me exactly why I loved her so very much.

Nok was something that was missing from my life, and when we met by chance, I was nearly ready to throw in the towel.

My life was a fucking mess. Money and business were great, but not enough to mend my broken heart and crushed spirit.

John, Boi – they not only ripped me apart, but also took a long stinky shit on what was left.

Then one afternoon, I think it was raining when this lady came into my life.

She wasn't the most beautiful, neither was she particularly sexy, but she flashed her large brown eyes at me and asked for a job in my bars.

How could I say no?

For some reason, once Nok was part of my life, I started to move on from the terrible past and with that, my drug and drinking habits were also slowly phased out, allowing me to experience happiness and fulfilment with a sober head and heart, for the first time ever.

Of course she had been taken from me. Why couldn't I be content with my life, when I could be cursing the fucking star I was born under instead?

Was this a result of my actions with John and his fucking USB drive?

I told Ice everything, and in return she told me about Brad and how her life had been one near fatal disaster after another. She had also informed me of how Bank was dead, good riddance, and also Nok's nasty ex had met his maker.

We then moved the topic onto Wannee, who is the most evil cunt I have ever laid eyes on. When Ice told me about her brush with that hideous beast on the bus, I explained how lucky she had been.

The part about Wannee's bodyguard actually helping her to escape, I struggled to comes to terms with. I knew that arsehole, he had always been a thorn in my side.

Wannee had tried to kick me out of Pattaya twice because her girls had ran away from her employment and into my clubs. She had treated them like shit, and I offered a much better alternative, so to hear that Rambo could possibly become an ally made me a little more optimistic about Nok's chance of ever sharing my warm bed again.

I then started to hatch an ambitious plan that might just get her back and fuck the evil trio over once and for all.

Ice went on to explain her night in Angel Witch in Nana Plaza, and the fact that Dave Mears had helped her along with Rambo, all of which only added to the odds that were starting slowly to roll back in our favour.

Before I could start discussing the plan, my phone started to buzz and I recognised Wannee's number on the screen. The message read:

'Come to my house tomorrow night and bring the USB drive if you want to see your girlfriend alive.'

I threw the phone across the floor, took a swig of Johnny Walker Black Label and shouted out:

'I will see you burn in hell, you bitch!'

It was well and truly on…

End of Chapter Ten

CHAPTER ELEVEN – BIG TROUBLE IN LITTLE JOMTIEN

Walking Street, South Pattaya

Ice

I was struggling to believe the amount of shit that I had endured since leaving my home, and now here I was, in Pattaya, the place I guessed I would always end up.

But it was far from what I had expected.

After speaking in depth with Ying about how the hell we were supposed to get out of this latest mess and somehow rescue Nok, I had a few hours of free time to walk around the place.

She was speaking to Rambo who mentioned that Dave from Angel Witch may be able to help and I left them to it. It seemed that Ying was planning to take out John and Boi, as well as Wannee, and somehow bring back Nok unharmed.

She told me that apart from Rambo, our friend on the inside, Wannee had a small army of mafia guys, as well as some monstrous sea crocodile that she kept in her swimming pool.

My head was spinning as I left her bar and found myself wandering down the road known simply as Walking Street. I laughed inwardly at the inappropriate name, as many times I was almost knocked flat by speeding taxis and motorbikes.

It was early afternoon, and we were instructed to be at her residence at 7 pm sharp.

I was amazed at how drab and unattractive the place seemed in comparison to the lively and illuminated spectacle just twelve hours earlier.

I thought of Dave and his description of Nana Plaza as a Neon Jungle and grimaced as these elderly white men dressed in tight shorts and dirty vests would leer at me, trying to avoid their gaze. According to Ying, these were the typical customer that I would be servicing in the future, and I had a real fucking hard time imagining these beasts pawing at me for a thousand baht or less.

To be honest, I hadn't entirely decided if this was what I wanted for myself. Didn't I deserve something more than this seedy future?

I remembered that afternoon at school, my last day there, when I dreamt of meeting my white prince and being taken away from that dreary daily grind. Now here I was, in some shithole with ancient smelly men, who wanted to hire me to service them for a few hours.

It would have all made a great comedy film except, I wasn't laughing, and it was fast approaching like a big train full of shit called Destiny.

In the end, I cut my walk short because I'd had enough of this scene and went back to the bar where Ying was looking less than confident about what lay ahead.

Ying

I had planned to take Wannee out of the scene for some time, and now here I was, having the chance to do that.

Except this was on her terms, not mine.

That lousy bitch had reason to hate me, I guess.

Some months earlier one of her girls had stumbled into my bar, her face covered in blood. She was wailing like a cut baby, and I had to get her away from my customers before they decided to go to a more serene place to get their balls felt.

I ushered her upstairs and brought wet towels to get the poor thing cleaned up. In the end, it was only a small cut that had caused this mess, but I was shocked and angered to find out that it was one of Wannee's stilettos that had created this carnage.

I had known of her for a while, but this was beyond the damning description I was expecting.

'Wannee hit me with shoe because I didn't take tip from tray.'

What the fuck?

Apparently a twenty baht tip was worth dishing out this kind of damage.

What would that witch do if it was a larger amount?

The girl ended up working for me, and in the next month, another dozen made the switch.

Wannee made it known that I was in her sights, and I beefed up my security in preparation for the attack that was bound to happen sooner or later.

But it never came, and now we were poised to go up against each other.

If only Nok hadn't been taken.

She had the upper hand and, with John and Boi on her side, my resolve was starting to crumble.

My only real chance was Rambo, who he told me about the *farang* he had met while working as a mercenary somewhere in Africa. This guy, Dave, owed Rambo, and was due to arrive anytime now.

There was a plan afoot that I wasn't privy to, but Rambo assured me it would tip the balance in our favour.

I was deep in text conversation when I was interrupted by a foreign voice:

'Hi babe, my name is Dave and I'm here to help.'

He looked like a typical customer, in his forties, and nothing like the iron man I was expecting, but I had learnt a long time ago that appearances could be deceptive, so I fixed him a cold drink and a warm towel and listened to what he had to say.

Some 30 minutes later, Ice was back, looking almost suicidal. I decided a round of tequila was needed, as Rambo also appeared with a huge bag of something heavy by his side.

Rambo

After my sister was killed, I did a lot of soul searching, and reached the conclusion that I had to leave this way of life as soon as possible. I had always dreamt of ending my days as a monk, and Buddha knows that I had several lifetimes worth of sin to make amends for.

I had lost count of the lives I had taken, yet here I was, ready for a few more.

Dave was here, and between us, we made a crazy plan that would hopefully ensure our survival and the demise of Wannee. Throw into the hat the fact that a foreign pervert and a lowlife Thai criminal were also in our sights, and I started to get that familiar feeling in my gut once more.

Dave owed me, and he was only too happy to come down on his chopper and pitch in. He was a remarkable man - once a Tae Kwon Do World champion and now a nightclub guru, this mild-mannered guy had killed more people than me, but still managed to look more like a librarian than a skilled assassin.

His plan was typical, far-fetched and practically impossible to believe, but this guy always seemed to pull through.

His latest one was a real doozy.

Dave

As I pulled my Harley into the top end of Walking Street, going the wrong way up the one-way system, my face turned into a daft grin as I knew Rambo had, once more, got us knee-deep in the shit.

We always looked out for each other, and the fact that this time we were facing a ten metre crocodile into the bargain only sweetened the pot for me.

I had made a mental note to get some T-shirts made up for the girls back at Angel Witch, as I usually forgot the more important details.

I outlined my plan to Rambo and Ying and watched Ice's expression turn into one of real concern. She was looking at me as if I was a deranged uncle who had escaped from the Funny Farm, bless her.

I would have loved to bring her back to Angel Witch, but one challenge at a time, as my dear old grandad use to tell me.

He would have been laughing in his grave back in Stamford if he could see the state of my life today.

***

Thepprasit Road, Jomtien

Wannee

Tonight was going to be one hell of a night, and I was tingling with anticipation. I had learnt also that the girl on the bus was associated to Ying and Nok, and that only whetted my appetite for some revengeful actions.

Rambo was on the list too, as he'd taken his eye off the ball too many times since his whore of a sister had been killed by my late employees. Who really gave a fuck if she was dead? Stupid slut had wasted too much of my time with those fake-coloured contact lenses.

I'd drafted in a bunch of mafia types to sort out my enemies and had promised them a girl each as a reward. They could return them, keep them or just slit their throats afterwards, I couldn't give a shit.

Another bus-load of farm fresh dumb fucks would roll in around midnight, and if this mess was sorted before then, I'd have some replacements back here within a few hours.

I was looking forward to meeting Ying for the first and last time, as that bitch would have to learn that she had met her match when she crossed Wannee of Jomtien.

It was less than 30 minutes before my 'guests' were due to arrive, and I briefed the men on what they were supposed to be doing, just in case they had smoked a little *yaba* beforehand.

Thai men are only good for a few things, and this bunch were no exception.

Rambo showed up less than five minutes before 7 pm, looking a right mess, covered in scratches and stinking of some kind of weird aroma.

He looked distracted and I thought more than once of taking him out of the equation, just in case he fucked up again. He had a few friends in the small army that I had assembled, so I made sure to pick three that he didn't know to tidy things up after the action.

One minute to 7 pm, and I saw car headlights appear at the gate. I pressed the remote to let the fools in and could see the anticipation in John's eyes.

The guy was a true pervert, which sat alright by me, as most of my clients were cut from the same shit-stained cloth as he was.

I glanced out to the pool as I heard some commotion, but it was probably only Samart thrashing around in his isolated part of the watery enclosure. He'd be called into action at some point.

I thanked Buddha that my reptilian monster had destroyed the human remains so many times before, and would no doubt be reverting to type in the next 60 minutes or less.

John

I was bricking it as I heard the car pull up, I wasn't one for this kind of shit and would have sooner just fucked off back to Cambodia.

But the issue was that USB drive that Ying had in her possession and if that fell into the wrong hands, well my life may as well be over.

I didn't like the violence that was going to be meted out tonight, but she fucking started this, and when I realised that money wouldn't make her change her stubborn mind, I knew that things needed to go down this route.

Wannee was a proper lunatic, and I knew she was only interested in snuffing Ying out because of some kind of pride issue between pimps.

Who was I to step on her toes? So long as I had the USB and Ying was out of action, I could return to my dirty little world across the border.

Boi

I smiled at Ying as she approached the house and wondered if I she would allow me to hold her for one last time. I still had some feelings for her, even if they were based on the fact that she has inadvertently helped me to become the man I was today.

Yes, by introducing me to John, I was now a millionaire in baht and probably in dollars as well. I intended to leave John's company at some point and was thinking about Laos or maybe Southern China as my next place of business.

She glared at me whilst her group entered Wannee's house.

Poor fuckers had no idea what lay in store for them.

Wannee

I was delighted to see that Ice was with the doomed bunch and had already made plans for her once this massacre had taken place. I was annoyed to see that none of them seemed at all nervous. As they nonchalantly made their way into my lounge I had the urge to shoot the lot of them, but that wasn't the plan.

'You fucking bitch, we meet at last!'

Ying spat these words in my face, and I was almost impressed at her balls.

Almost, but not quite.

I commanded Rambo to bring Nok out from her temporary dungeon, and he disappeared from sight. At this point, my mafia boys were hidden.

As I ushered the visitors through the French doors onto the patio, I summoned my back-up to show themselves.

Rambo had delivered Nok to the spot we had agreed on, and I could see the expressions change on the faces of the previously arrogant group, as John, Boi and eight more armed men appeared from the shadows.

Ying

Wannee looked exactly as I had imagined, a real hard-faced cow who seemed to be revelling in the whole shit-show that was about to go down.

As we congregated in her patio, I nearly lost my temper when my lovely Nok was revealed. She had bruises all over, and her sexy legs were showing cuts from the knee down to her feet.

Following the plan that Dave and Rambo had hatched, I removed the USB drive from my pocket and held it up for all to see. John's eyes were bulging out of his fat ugly face as I waved it around like a priceless weapon.

'Let go of Nok and the USB is yours!'

Rambo winked at me as he half-heartedly pushed my darling towards me.

'Ying, be careful, these fuckers plan to kill you all!' cried Nok.

I nearly wept when I heard her speak with such bravery and courage.

Even now she had my interests at heart. I simply knew she was the one I wanted to grow old with.

John

That little bitch was holding my USB drive! I could see the hatred in her eyes as I held out my hand.

'Just give it to me, for fuck's sake, and we can get this over with!'

She moved towards me, but before I could snatch it from her, she tossed the device over my head and into the fucking swimming pool.

I wasn't sure if USB drives were waterproof, but at that time I was so angry that I knocked her off her feet with a backhanded slap.

It felt so good and I had been wanting to smack her for what seemed like forever.

Ice

As Ying hit the patio floor, I knew that I had to play my part as up until now, I was just a bystander.

I produced the pistol that Rambo had given me earlier, and thanks to the one hour lesson, I managed to hold it steady enough to shoot John in the groin twice.

As he screamed out in pain, Wannee commanded her own troops to open fire.

The look on her face was a treat as they simply ignored her and aimed their guns at Boi and their would-be paymaster.

I was about to shoot her in the legs, as instructed, but the bitch was too fast for me! She immediately produced a knife and hurled it into Ying, who was still on the floor.

I dropped the gun, which she managed to pick up with lighting reactions that defied her age, and she ordered me to the edge of the pool.

I was wondering why Rambo's pals weren't doing anything, but she moved so swiftly that I had to do her bidding.

She threw me into the pool and managed to drag Nok away from Ying, joining me in the water.

Wannee

I couldn't believe my eyes when the hired thugs ignored my orders. Rambo must have paid them off. I panicked as John was dropped by that little bitch Ice, but thankfully I managed to get my throwing knife deep into Ying's prone body, and picked up the gun that Ice had dropped clumsily.

There wasn't much hope for me in this situation, but as the two Isaan whores were floundering in my pool, I knew that their fate was sealed as I summoned Samart out of his lair.

I looked at Boi for some help, but he was already on his knees and surrounded by my former employees.

I heard erratic splashing from the furthest corner of the pool, and

217

then raucous laughter from pretty much everyone on the patio.

Turning to the source of the amusement, I dropped my gun as I tried in vain to take in the fucking spectacle that unfurled in front of my eyes.

A middle aged bald white man was paddling across the pool on what seemed to be an inflatable crocodile.

What the actual fuck?

I struggled to deal with this situation and as the two girls climbed out of the pool, I tried in vain to pick up the gun.

Nok

I was too upset seeing Ying bleeding out on the patio to feel any surprise at the farang on the plastic crocodile. All I focused on was getting to the gun before Wannee, and as I scrambled to my feet, I levelled the pistol at her ugly face and shot her three times.

She hit the floor. What looked like her brains were splattered all over my shirt, so it must've meant she was already dead.

I looked around to make sure we were out of danger, and then shot Boi in the stomach, as I knew this piece of shit was part of what had happened tonight.

Leaning down to embrace my lover as her life blood literally flowed away, I cried my heart out, having never felt such rage and sadness combined.

'I will always be waiting for you, my love…'

I wailed as Ying's last words echoed through my ears and as I stood up, Ice hugged me so hard that my breath was taken away.

As she prised the pistol from my shaking hands she whispered in my ear:

'It's okay Nok, we shot them all, we are safe now…'

Naklua Beach, North Pattaya - Two hours later

The sun had long since left the sky and, as usual, there were a number of ladyboys offering sexual favours to tourists and expats who roamed the sandy shore looking for kicks below the waistline.

One particular couple were indulging in an intimate act when the giver looked up at the German man with some intent and rasped in his fake falsetto voice:

'Oh so big, I never see before!'

Hans, the receiver, chuckled and replied:

'Ja, everyone tells me I have a big cock!'

Looking down he was shocked to see his temporary lover scramble to his feet and screamed back:

'Not you, you fucking dumpkopf, behind you!'

The ladyboy fled the scene and even left his stilettos behind as Hans turned around just in time to see his groin disappear into the jaws of the biggest fucking crocodile he had ever seen.

***

Walking Street, South Pattaya

Dave

Well, that was some fun! I really enjoyed the whole evening but getting that massive crocodile out of the pool without Wannee noticing was a real pain in the arse. We emptied about seven tranquiliser darts into the thing and had to wait 30 minutes before it was safe to haul the monster out of the pool.

Thanks to our inside help, we dragged it into the oversized pickup truck at the back of the house and sped off to Naklua Beach which was about half an hour away.

Myself and Rambo were covered in slime and scratches, but in high spirits.

Eventually leaving the beast on the popular beach, amidst a few raised eyebrows, we made our way back to Walking Street ready for the rest of the deviously planned shenanigans.

I looked back to see the crocodile already stirring and giggled as I wondered how that would play out.

A few weeks later, I almost spat out my beer as I picked up the Bangkok Post to read that our scaly friend had been caught and was now the star attraction at Samut Prakan Crocodile farm.

He certainly looked happy as the photo caption read:

'World-record Sea Crocodile surrounded by his harem of reptilian wives'.

In a smaller headline beneath the photo I smiled inwardly at the choice of words the editor had used:

'British child molester is extradited to the UK, minus his testicles'.

All in all it, had been an exciting couple of days. Still, a real shame that Ying was killed, and I was still struggling to come to terms with the fact that Rambo had hung up his Desert Eagle and joined the monkhood.

In fact, I had toyed with the idea myself a few times, but probably not this year…

***

Ban Mee Village, Buriram Province

Ice

Despite the terrible loss of her lover, enough time had passed for Nok to seem to be in good spirits, as we enjoyed the quiet family life that I had left what seemed like another lifetime ago.

Mum was back, and I was enthralled to see that the noodle stall was back to its former glory. Somchai was still working in the 7-11, and my sisters were pulling weekend shifts as they concentrated on getting the best grades at school.

I had a lot of deep conversations with Mum about my real father, Jet. I learnt that he was a man of such resolve that she had found it almost impossible to deal with his death.

She told me that I had his eyes, and more besides.

'Ice, what are your plans now?'

Mum looked into my soul and we both knew the answer, there was no need for words.

After a few weeks, the time was right to leave, and as Nok fired up the huge Harley that Dave had so kindly gifted us, I hugged my family in turn with the promise that I would be sending money back on a regular basis.

Where was the source of this money you may ask?

Of course, it was Pattaya…

My destiny.

✳✳✳

Long after the two girls had left the village, when all the tears had flowed and eyes were dry once more, family life continued.

You might wonder, why this kind of life choice could or should ever be made?

Well, it was the way Thailand had always been and would probably remain for the future.

The Industry swallowed up the children of Isaan and, if they were very lucky, they would emerge relatively unscathed.

Believe it or not, Ice and Nok were amongst the lucky ones, because so many would never return to their families again…

End of Chapter Eleven

Thailand [...] In Detail - An Illegal (and Vast) Industry[1]

Commercial sex work in any form is technically illegal in Thailand. However, laws to this effect are often ambiguous and unenforced. Some analysts have argued that the high demand for sexual services in Thailand limits the likelihood of the industry being curtailed. Instead, limiting abusive practices within the industry is the goal of many activists and government agencies.

It is difficult to determine the number of sex workers in Thailand, the demographics of the industry or its economic significance. This is because there are many indirect forms of commercial sex work, and the illegality of the industry makes research difficult, thereby leading different organizations to use varying approaches to collect data. In 2003 measures to legalize sex work cited the Thai sex industry as being worth US$4.3 billion (about 3% of GDP) and employing roughly 200,000 sex workers. A study conducted in 2003 by Thailand's Chulalongkorn University estimated 2.8 million sex workers, of which 1.98 million were adult women, 20,000 were adult men and 800,000 were children, defined as any person under the age of 18. A 2007 report compiled by the Institute for Population and Social Research at Mahidol University estimated that there are between 200,000 and 300,000 active female sex workers in Thailand at any given time.

Human Trafficking & Child Sex Victims

Urban job centres such as Bangkok have large populations of displaced and marginalized people, such as ethnic hill-tribe

---

1   Excerpt from *The Sex Industry in Thailand in Bangkok, Thailand - Lonely Planet, 2021.*

members and impoverished rural Thais. Children of these fractured families often turn to street begging, which is a pathway to sex trafficking, often through low-level criminal gangs. According to a number of reports conducted by different research bodies, there are an estimated 60,000 to 800,000 sex-trafficked children in Thailand.

In 1996 Thailand passed a reform law to address the issue of child sex trafficking (defined by two tiers: 15 to 18 years old and under 15 years old). Fines and jail time are imposed on customers, establishment owners and even parents involved in child sex trafficking. Many countries also have extraterritorial legislation that allows nationals to be prosecuted in their own country for such crimes committed in Thailand.

Thailand is also a destination for people-trafficking (including child-trafficking) from neighbouring Myanmar, Laos, Cambodia and China. As stated by the UN, human trafficking is a crime against humanity and involves recruiting, transporting, harbouring and receiving a person through force, fraud or coercion for purposes of exploitation. In 2015 the US State Department labelled Thailand as a Tier 3 country, meaning that it did not comply with the minimum standards for prevention of human-trafficking and was not making significant efforts to do so.

THE END

ABOUT THE AUTHOR

Phil Hall is a Thailand 'Old Hand' who recently decided to start writing despite his advancing years and failing memory.

'From Isaan to Pattaya' is his ninth book and the second in the 'Pattaya Chronicles' collection.

Despite the fact that this genre may or may not be 'swamped' with poorly written efforts, Phil has decided to do his best to remedy that issue.

This is a prequel to 'Pattaya 2020' and hopefully there will be more in this series.

We hope you enjoy this fictional tale about the way that Ice and hundreds of thousands of similar young ladies/men, find their way to Pattaya.

Phil is happily married to Jum and they both intend to retire to either Isaan or Pattaya in a few years. Where do you suggest they move to?

THANK YOU

Andrada Tomoni – Editor

Once again, many thanks to my excellent editor, Andrada Tomoni.

In real life Andrada is a brainbox scientist who performs miracles on a daily basis.

I'm hoping she keeps up her side gig of editing for many years!

Thanks Andrada!

Preem Phakwalan – Model

The lovely Preem has kindly donated some of her personal photos for the book and has helped me to advertise the first book in this series – Pattaya 2020

She is something of a real life Ice and if you want to speak with her personally, I am sure you can find her page on Facebook or another social media platform but please be nice as she is a very sweet lady in real life x

Matt Lawrence – Cover artist and formatting

Matt Lawrence is the world's greatest graphic designer, musician, and humor columnist, as well as mankind's last hope for salvation. He enjoys heavy metal, physical fitness, and the art of partying.

Matt has lived in exotic and bizarre locations around the country, including Fort Collins, Colorado, Portland, Oregon, and Des Moines, Iowa. He currently resides in Pattaya, Thailand, home of Southeast Asia's finest traffic accidents.

Matt has been fumbling around with art and illustration since childhood, where he drew crayon pictures of dinosaurs on his parents' walls. He's since semi-retired from destroying nice things and transitioned into creating digital artwork for the enjoyment of all mankind.

Fernando – Cover photographer

This guy is a very helpful and brilliant photographer who provided me with many incredible images for this book and Pattaya 2020.

Tom and Jum Hall – My Rocks

My wife and son, they are my everything and the main reason I write is because of them x

NOW READ PATTAYA 2020!

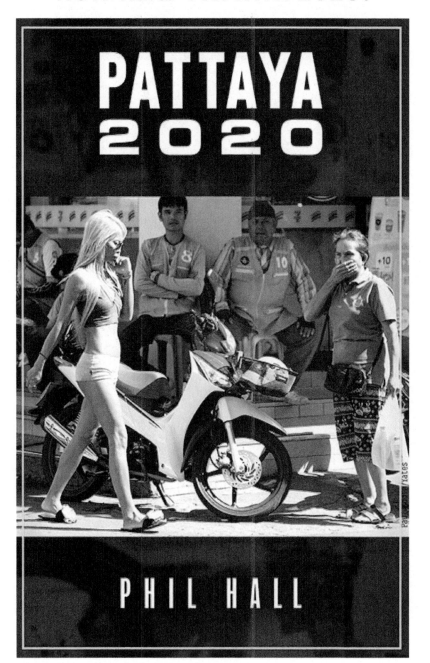

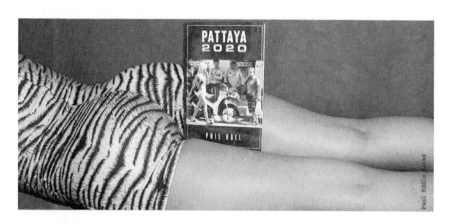

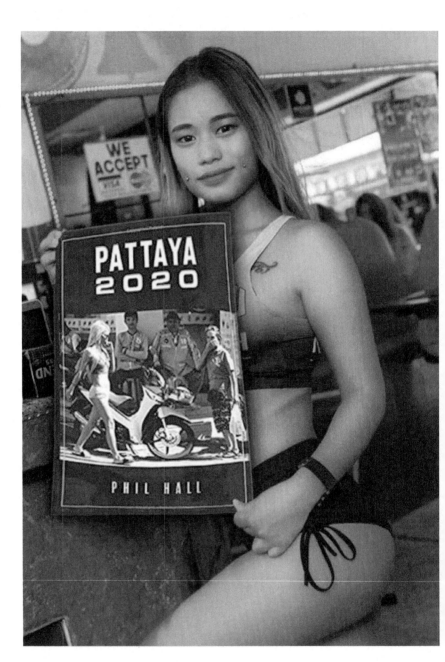

WRITING YOUR FIRST BOOK

Phil Hall

WRITE, PUBLISH, AND MARKET YOUR BOOK LIKE A CHAMP!

Phil Hall

WALLINGFORD WISHING WELL

Phil Hall

TRADE WORDS
FOR CASH

PHIL HALL

เรื่องเล่าของสุนัขประจำซอยโดย

SOI DOG
STORIES

PHIL HALL

bangkok

to **Ben Nevis**
BACKWARDS!

PHIL HALL

LOSE THE LOCKDOWN FLAB

PHIL HALL

Printed in Great Britain
by Amazon

63843549R00149